The Management Mind Field

AVOIDING THE PITFALLS OF CORPORATE POLITICS

This book is dedicated to my parents,

Angelo and Josephine.

Without their unwavering love,

support, and the sense of discipline and commitment

they instilled in me, completing

this project

would not have been possible.

The Management Mind Field

AVOIDING THE PITFALLS OF CORPORATE POLITICS

BY TONY PARADISO

Published by:

NYK Publishing
P.O. Box 148
Amherst, NH 03031

Published by:

NYK Publishing
P.O. Box 148
Amherst, NH 03031

Cover & book design by Marlitt Dellabough
Edited by Judi Gardner

Printed in the United States of America

Library of Congress Control Number: 2002091153
ISBN 0-9717429-3-6

Contents

Introduction: A Matter of Perspective   1

PART ONE · THE SOUL

1   No Good Deed Goes Unpunished   11
2   The Dot-com Debacle   20
3   As Luck Would Have It   31
4   The Price of Politics   47

PART TWO · THE HEART

5   The Life Blood of Business   57
        It Ain't Rocket Science But ...   67
6   Optimism Can be Hazardous to Your Health   72
7   Image is Everything Including Expensive   84
8   The Internet: Fact Versus Fiction   96
9   David and Goliath Parts I & II   107
        Got Music?   125

PART THREE · THE MIND

10   Where Egos Fly   133
11   Accentuate the Negative   149
12   Who Do You Work For?   158
13   A Man's Got To Know His Limitations:
        The Demise of the XFL   161
14   Consensus Management: To Serve or Protect?   169
15   A Mirror's Reflection   175
16   Rules of the Game   180
17   The Moral of the Story   185
Epilogue: What's at the Bottom of that Cracker Jack Box   189

A Matter of Perspective

There are many challenges to writing a book. One of the most notable, particularly for a first-time author, is the nagging question, *who am I to write a book?* If I've learned nothing else in my career, it is this simple truth: having value doesn't automatically translate into success. The best people rarely run for political office, the best products don't always become market leaders, and the best business minds don't necessarily rise to the top.

So who am I? On the surface, this seems like a straightforward question. But who anyone "is" is a matter of perspective. Perspective is a critical factor in business and in life. It may not garner much attention in business books or in the classroom; however it is arguably one of the most important issues in understanding how to successfully navigate the complex mazes of the business world.

To illustrate the impact perspective can have, let's answer the question of who I am from several different perspectives.

If you asked one of my family members they'd probably tell you I'm someone who never seems satisfied, always searching for more, unable to settle down. Translation: I didn't go the traditional route of marrying and having children. A brash and cocky man who thinks he knows everything and never knows when to shut up. Actually, I'm that to a lot of people.

To the average citizen, I'd likely be considered a highly successful businessman, earning a six-figure salary in one of the most dynamic industries in the world. Someone who has been lucky enough to make good money, travel the world, and obtain many of life's comforts. A person who has pursued and attained the American dream.

In contrast, to the world's elite, I would be considered a nobody. A somewhat obscure marketing person who has achieved senior level management positions with mid-sized high tech companies. I'm not a Bill Gates or a Donald Trump.

But who am I from my perspective? Got about an hour? Just kidding. I'll be brief.

I consider myself one of the top marketing executives in high tech. I've worked with no less than eight market leaders achieving the level of vice president along the way. My consulting services have been retained by some of the industry's premier organizations including AT&T, Intel, Xerox, Soros, and Ziff-Davis.

While in my twenties, I had already risen to director level status with responsibility for a product line worth over $200 million. And that was when $200 million was a lot of money. Early in my career I was regularly quoted in trade press around the world and my name was fairly well recognized throughout the industry. A major industry publication once even labeled me a pillar of strength. On more than one occasion, while working for relatively small organizations, I successfully battled industry giants including Microsoft and Intel.

I was on the fast track, destined to become one of the industry's elite executives. I could have easily been *someone*. Or as Marlon Brando so eloquently put it in *On the Waterfront*, "I coulda been a contenda." That was before I realized there were more important things than money and power. I chose another path, one that will become clear in these pages. But don't worry. The book isn't about me.

The point is, who anyone "is" is relative. A Buddhist monk wouldn't automatically consider a millionaire successful. That's a capitalist society standard. We consider achieving the highest levels within business and politics a measure of success. By our standards money and social status are valid measures. But should they be the sole measures? What should be as important, is how one gets there.

This, in part, is what this book is about. It is a journey through the corporate world as seen through the eyes of someone who had the opportunity to *join the club*, but chose not to. It is a brutally honest account of the underlying cultural and political influences that drive corporate America. It examines the choices anyone striving to achieve the highest levels in business will face.

What qualifies me to write this and why should you believe what I say?

Having experienced business as both an employee and a consultant I have witnessed the business process from every angle with over 20 companies. Most people spend their entire career with a handful of companies. This has a tendency to limit the breadth of their business knowledge. There are many ways to *skin the cat* of business and I've been exposed to many more than most.

Viewing business from a marketing perspective provides a working knowledge of every aspect of business, from finance, to operations, to sales. I have found that marketing is the only discipline within an organization that routinely interfaces with every department in a company. Rather than having a narrow view, marketing sees the entire picture.

Further, the organizational level on which I operated was singularly positioned to interact with all other organizational levels. This included being privy to the inner workings of senior management in the course of developing corporate and product strategies. And, at the other end of the spectrum, it meant interfacing with lower organizational levels to facilitate the implementation of those strategies.

Observing business from every perspective has allowed me to develop a comprehensive understanding of the entire range of business dynamics – somewhat like understanding every piece of a jigsaw puzzle and how they fit together. This is a perspective even many CEOs often do not possess.

Reinforcing this broad organizational background is an equally diverse career path. Today's world is one of specialization. Most people focus on a specific aspect of an industry. I don't personally find that intellectually rewarding. That's a sophisticated way of saying I have a short attention span. As a consequence, I've had the good fortune to explore nearly the full breadth of the technology industry and then some.

Arguably, my product and market expertise are second to none. In an almost three decade career, I've managed a plethora of products. While still in my teens, my first job was as an assistant factory foreman with a school supply manufacturer. Since entering the high tech fray, the products I've marketed run the gamut from PCs, to enhancement products, printers, IBM and Macintosh software, e-commerce Web sites, Internet content, video in numerous forms, telecommunications, market research, and field service. And for a recent consulting assignment I even spent the better part of a year managing a children's nutrition company. I kid you not. Pun intended.

This path has provided a unique and all-encompassing view of the world of business. It could be said I possess one of the most comprehensive business perspectives at both the micro organizational level, and macro industrial level. The byproduct is having observed and analyzed the intricate inter-dependencies that comprise all industries as well as the impact those interdependencies have on individual companies and markets.

This can only be achieved through direct experience. All industries are a collage of individual markets. In the case of high tech, the markets consist of PCs, software, networking, communications, and information. These markets create the platforms, the software that runs on the platforms, the communications infrastructure that connects the platforms, and the content distributed to users of the platforms. Not many people experience them all.

As I pen these words, I am fully conscience of the fine line between conveying my credentials and appearing to do nothing more than brag. You may think this is merely a case of blowing smoke. Isn't this what marketing does for a living? Actually no. That's part of sales' job description. All I can say is the only way to determine if I know what I'm talking about is to read the book.

In reading the book I ask you to do one thing. Assume I know what I'm talking about until I give you reason to think otherwise. With two business degrees and twenty-eight years of hands-on experience I've been preparing most of my adult life for this moment. Not that I realized it at the time. It wasn't my intent to acquire such a diverse background or to write a book for that matter. But in retrospect, my career has put me in an ideal position to do so.

You'll quickly realize this is no ordinary business book. Unlike most business books, this one is written in plain English. It strives to simplify the complex rather than complicate the simple. Think of it as Dilbert on steroids. But instead of just poking fun at reality, we examine the serious side and offer ways to improve it. You might even be in for a surprise or two along the way. You'll certainly experience a new perspective; one that will make you think, prepare you to recognize the signs of healthy and unhealthy companies, and allow you to better understand the mindset and motivations of management.

The book is divided into three parts:

- *The Soul* examines the core beliefs that drive the business world along with its sense of ethics or lack thereof.
- *The Heart* discusses the increasingly important role marketing plays and examines a number of key marketing concepts.
- *The Mind* addresses the psychological influences of management and debates widely held management philosophies.

The goal is to impart business insights useful to everyone at all levels in a company. It is a *how to* book in a sense, but not in the normal sense. I admit, I haven't read many traditional business books written by so-called experts pontificating about how to successfully run a business. I tried reading *In Search of Excellence* once. It bored me to tears. But I've read enough to know this one doesn't fit the mold.

The book does not attempt to explain the *mechanics* of business. Communicating the mechanical processes is something business schools and a myriad of textbooks do well. In fact, it may be the only thing you can learn from these sources.

The aim is to provide an understanding of the *real* business world, the *essence* of business, and to offer insight into the political, personal, and cultural underpinnings that impact day-to-day business life. This knowledge is intended to assist in understanding the motives behind decisions and how those motives can impact individual careers. It will also assist in recognizing the key indicators that determine whether a company is likely to succeed or fail. All of this will allow you to make better career choices.

We'll also examine some of the facets that comprise the art and science of marketing. But this isn't a book about marketing per se. It is a book about business as seen through the eyes of a marketing executive. The benefits and necessity of having this perspective will become evident as you read.

If you permit me to momentarily suspend reality, there is also the hope the book will act as a catalyst to alter the mentality of business and to restructure its priorities. I would like nothing more than to be a small part of enhancing the ethical conduct and reward system of business. Why? It's certainly not because I'm a champion of the oppressed. That is not who I am. My purpose for changing the culture of business is to increase the long-term success and profitability of business. The benefits of this cultural change would extend to everyone and take our economy and country to new heights. And oh yes, the icing on the cake is it would serve to improve our moral climate. That's what I'd like the book to accomplish if you allow me to suspend reality.

In light of the pitiful conduct exhibited by key members of the Enron management team, the need to alter the values of business management has never been more necessary. The opinions and observations in this book were not developed with Enron in mind. The references to Enron were added during the editing process. However, as you read, be aware that many of the issues I raise are at the very heart of what caused Enron's collapse. Enron is an extreme example of management misconduct, but understand similar behavior exists in almost every company to varying degrees.

Lastly, I'd like to believe reading these words will be entertaining in addition to being informative.

So, let the journey begin.

PART ONE · THE SOUL

CHAPTER ONE

No Good Deed
Goes Unpunished

Most people are familiar with the phrase no good deed goes unpunished. It's not the most positive saying in the world but it epitomizes one of the biggest challenges everyone faces in building a career. It is at the core of what is perhaps the central issue of corporate life: the choice between what is right for the company versus what is right for the individual.

This is my favorite story. It's as much a testament to my sense of irony as it is to the value placed on the lessons that can be learned. For these reasons, and in an effort to engage you early, I decided to lead with it. First impressions are as important for products and companies as they are for people.

A number of years ago I was hired by the world leader in videoconferencing. They were forming a new division to migrate the company's technology to the PC platform. My role was director of marketing with worldwide responsibilities for all the division's marketing functions.

The company had, historically, sold large systems for use in conference rooms. At the time, these systems typically cost between $25,000 and $50,000. Our goal was to take that technology and develop a $6,000 PC add-on. The add-on would turn the PC into a videoconferencing terminal. The PC-based system would perform the same basic functions as the big systems, but at a lower level of quality.

The company was based in New England and I was relocating from California. Those familiar with the two regions know there are major differences in the mindset and approach to business. I was hired partly because I was a *West Coast guy* with an aggressive, *take-no-prisoners* attitude. This style is more reflective of a start-up, particularly in a rapidly shifting industry like high tech. Though this company was established, the creation of the new division was like forming a start-up making my addition to the team a logical one.

On my second day on the job, I was invited to attend a senior-level meeting to review a presentation being made by the company's ad agency. I thought, "This is pretty cool." The president, CFO, and division heads were all attending, so the meeting would provide immediate exposure to the senior management team. Being asked to participate was definitely a positive thing. Or so I thought.

The ad agency was presenting concepts for a corporate branding campaign. Now, branding campaigns are tricky business. Successful ones require significant amounts of money and must be sustained over a relatively long period of time. One year is the absolute minimum. Realistically, it takes two to four years for a message to sink in. This is particularly true when a company has no identity, as was the case here.

The company was of modest size with annual revenues approaching $250 million; however they had experienced very healthy growth in recent years. All signs were positive and everyone believed the market was poised to explode.

This combination of factors often leads to companies attempting to initiate some sort of branding campaign. When companies grow to the $250 million to $500 million mark they begin to think about what they need to do to get to $1 billion in revenues. Healthy growth over a number of years often results in management beginning to feel their oats. They think, *We're on a roll. It's time to brand ourselves.*

Bad idea. Most of the time it's more than a little premature. Even a $500 million company will struggle with the financial investment necessary to execute a successful branding campaign. The one exception may be a company sitting on a mountain of cash from a stock offering.

What frequently happens, though, is the collective ego of the management team comes into play. They want to get the company to the next level and think the best way to do that is to spend lots of money to tell the world who they are. That aptly describes the circumstances of this and many other companies.

The meeting was held in the boardroom and there must have been 20 people in attendance, with the ad agency providing the usual entourage. They were a well-known New York firm who took the assignment when others had refused. Other agencies had turned the project down because in their collective opinion the $5 million budget wasn't nearly enough to achieve the objective. For whatever reason, this agency accepted and undoubtedly did their best to develop a viable campaign.

The corporate marketing team was also in attendance. The campaign was their *baby*. They were driving hard to make it happen for a number of reasons, not the least of which was the personal satisfaction of implementing and managing such an effort. But there was a problem. Most of the people in corporate marketing had very little marketing experience.

The VP of Marketing had come from the finance department. She was a bright woman, that wasn't the issue. The problem was she was not a marketing person. She was, however, a long-time and respected employee. She had helped the company raise much-needed capital in the early days. Word was the company didn't think she had the horsepower to be CFO, but in an effort to reward her for her contribution, she was slotted in the marketing role.

Unfortunately, she didn't have the training, the necessary experience, or the *feel* for the position. The staff she had assembled hadn't come from solid marketing backgrounds either. Collectively, they were not equipped to handle something as sophisticated as a branding campaign.

The big moment was upon us. The ad agency began with the usual BS to lay the groundwork for their ideas. Then they unveiled their plan. The strategy was to spend $4 million of the $5 million in airport dioramas. Those are the billboards plastered in the terminals of every airport in the country.

Brilliant! As a videoconferencing company, one of our marketing strategies was to sell the product as an alternative to travel. Our target market consisted of business people who wanted to avoid the expense of getting on a plane without sacrificing the ability to communicate visually. It made perfect sense. Millions of business people and decision makers walk through airports every year. In theory, a large number of them would see our ads. A stroke of genius! We would get millions and millions of impressions for a mere $4 million. By the way, an impression in ad-speak refers to how many people walk through the airport. It does not refer to how many people actually read the ad. Therein lies the rub.

Being eager to impress, and not the least bit bashful to offer an opinion, I asked a simple question: *Who reads these things?* I never did. As a business traveler my goal was to get in and out of the airport as quickly as possible. I hardly noticed any of the dioramas. The only ones I could recall were from familiar companies or because some graphic element caught my eye.

But the proposed ads would have no color or graphics. They would be comprised solely of text. Even if you believed airport billboards were viable, the execution was flawed. There was simply nothing in the ads to catch a reader's attention in a hectic and sensory overloaded environment like an airport.

You might assume the agency would have been prepared

to address this issue. You might even expect them to have come armed with reams of focus-group studies proving a very high percentage of business travelers studied these dioramas to death. You also might have thought the corporate marketing team would have asked the same question well before the meeting.

But alas, this was not the case. All the agency could fall back on was to quote the number of impressions and to state how other companies had successfully run similar campaigns. Of course, they couldn't cite any specific company or provide any detailed data regarding successful results.

In the spirit of cooperation they did offer to conduct research into the matter. The only catch was it would drastically delay the project and would significantly eat into our already tight budget. The cost of actually proving or disproving the idea would range between $100,000 and $250,000. But they could do it, God bless them!

As you would imagine, my little question turned out to be more than a little disruptive. Quite innocently, well, not so innocently, I had firmly planted the seeds of doubt among the senior management team. I didn't know it at the time but the CFO was doing cartwheels in his head. Being a good little bean counter he was looking for any excuse to scuttle the campaign and put the $5 million back on the bottom line.

Needless to say, the campaign was never executed, which was a good thing. It was premature for the company to think of branding itself. Even if the timing was right, this campaign certainly wasn't going to work. The company would have flushed $5 million down the proverbial toilet.

I'm thinking, "wow, my second day with the company and I saved them five million bucks. This has to be good for a couple of feathers in my cap. I'm a lock to become a VP. "

Was I ever wrong. I did score some points with the CFO. He befriended me and helped me during my tenure - at least up to the point where it impacted him personally. But that was nowhere near enough to compensate for the wrath of the corporate marketing group, and in particular, the VP. From that day forward I was public enemy *numero uno*. I had to be eliminated.

What's the moral of the story? There isn't one. I just like the story. I'm kidding. There is a moral. In fact, there are a number of morals.

First and foremost, *being right doesn't necessarily count for squat in the business world.* This is probably the most important lesson anyone can learn. That is not to say being right has no value. Of course it does. In most cases being right is a good thing. But it's not an automatic. To build a successful career it is critical to recognize when being right may not be personally beneficial.

This was a classic example. There was no question stopping the campaign was the right thing to do for the company; however there was also no question being the catalyst behind scuttling it would lead to personal political problems.

This leads to the second and third lessons. *Be aware of the political climate if you hope to avoid political blunders.* And *understand that sometimes an employee's influence can extend well beyond his or her position.*

I was partially aware of the political climate prior to the meeting but did not fully comprehend the personal dynamics. I had totally miscalculated the influence held by the VP of marketing. Although that *role* was not influential, the *person* filling the role was. It stemmed from her long history and the significant contribution she had made on the financial side of the business.

Would I have changed my behavior if I had recognized the issues in advance? No. It wouldn't have mattered in the least to me. It never has. Which is why I'm writing this book instead of running a major technology company. But that's me. I have always been fully prepared to suffer the personal consequences of doing what I believed to be right.

Frankly, in this case, political awareness or diplomacy wasn't likely to alter the results. Being new to the company made me an outsider. Compounding the problem was the fact my roots were in California and New York. New Englanders are wonderful people but they are not quick to embrace people from other parts of the country. I might as well have had 666 tattooed to my forehead with a background like mine. New York and California, it doesn't get any worse from the perspective of a native New Englander.

This is something to be cognizant of when considering a new company. Is there a cultural match? Will the company embrace someone from a different region or background? Or will it be difficult to assimilate? The answers to these questions may determine how rewarding the job will be and how successful you will become.

More to the point of no good deed going unpunished, this particular situation was not a matter of being right or wrong or being diplomatic. It was a matter of hurt feelings and the perception of *trespassing on someone's turf.*

How a person reacts when confronted with this type of decision is a personal choice. I would not necessarily recommend following my lead. Everyone has to make his/her own determination as to what is best, personally. So I won't presume to tell you what is right or wrong.

What I can do is provide some advice to better prepare you to make the decision. It comes down to understanding the *lay of the land.* You can begin doing this before and during the interview process. Even though you won't know exactly what a company is like until you get there, try and find out as much as you can. Don't be afraid to ask questions about the senior management team, the people you anticipate interfacing with, and the people in the department you may join.

Check the company's Web site or other company information (press releases, annual reports etc.) to review the backgrounds of the management team and gather other pertinent information. Ask questions during the interview process. Once you've joined a company, engage people in casual conversations to get a sampling of perspectives regarding the political and cultural environment.

Specifically, it would be useful to know things like: Where did the management team work before? What were their responsibilities and how many years of experience do they have? How long have they been with the company? And as important, who have they worked with in the past? This last question will offer significant insight into *coalitions* that may exist within a company. If people have a history of working together in other companies, it may indicate they are aligned. Alienating one may mean alienating all. You get the idea.

The best source of information is obviously from people you know. If you're fortunate enough to know someone in the company or who once worked for the company, find out what you can. When you do, temper what they tell you with the understanding everyone's perspective is subjective. You need to put what they say in the proper context. For example, their views will be impacted by what department they work for or where they are or were within the organizational structure. Their perspective will also be affected by the relationship they have or had with their superiors. All these factors need to be taken into consideration.

If you're seeking a position in a department such as marketing, ask about marketing's historic role and the company's goals for marketing. Try and determine if the company is marketing-driven or driven by other departments like engineering or sales. If there are multiple marketing organizations, investigate how these organizations interact and which ones have the greatest control.

All of this will help paint a picture of how key managers might think and react in a particular situation. This will help you understand what challenges may exist in performing your role and will allow you to identify and understand the potential ramifications of your actions.

Corporate politics and personal motivations play an enormous role in the decision-making process in almost every company. At some point, if you hope to rise in the corporate hierarchy you're going to be faced with a decision similar to the one I faced. Will you do what you believe is right or will you do the politically expedient thing? It is an age-old dilemma. Be prepared to face it more than once in your career if your goal is to *play with the big boys.*

Not the most upbeat way to start. But thinking about this story still makes me chuckle. If you harbored any thoughts this book would be like any other business book you might have read, now you know better. Enjoy the ride.

CHAPTER TWO

The Dot-com Debacle

The dot-com, or should we say debt-com experience, serves to illustrate another important business influence: GREED. Greed of course is one of the great American motivators. Despite having negative connotations, when properly applied, greed can be a good thing.

If I were greed, I would be thinking about getting a new agent. Being one of the seven deadly sins can't be good. It's the equivalent of being on the worst dressed list for words. I mean there are only seven words that made it to *deadly* sin status. This has to pose more than a small public relations problem.

Greed did attempt to improve its image in the late '80s by getting the charismatic Michael Douglas to try to convince the world it was in fact a good thing. In the movie *Wall Street*, the Douglas character Gordon Gekko, tried to explain the rationale for the benefits of greed. Unfortunately Gordo wasn't a very sympathetic figure, particularly after his empire collapsed because of a little thing called insider trading. Well, I guess Oliver Stone wasn't really trying to espouse the virtues of greed.

Neither am I. Despite believing greed can serve to motivate people in a positive way, it does have the habit of getting out of control. No better example of that exists than what transpired with the dot-coms.

In the case of the dot-coms, greed wasn't a problem isolated to Wall Street. It consumed everyone including venture capitalists (VCs), the snot-nosed 20-somethings who actually thought they knew how to run a company, and everyone who bought even a single share of stock in a company without the slightest thought about whether or not that company had a viable business model.

How it all got started is a blur. It happened so fast. I do remember that early on I likened it to a high-stakes game of musical chairs. You definitely didn't want to be standing when the music stopped. Unfortunately, most of the people left standing were average citizens caught up in the frenzy and hype of becoming overnight millionaires. They not only lost their chairs, many of them lost their shirts, shoes, and worse.

I, for one, would have felt much better if the VCs and Wall Street types took the hit. But of course, I doubt most of them actually lost much money on the deal. Not that I have anything against VCs and Wall Street. Wait, actually I do, but that's not why I believe they should have felt the pain. They should have taken the financial hit because they could have, and should have prevented the situation from happening in the first place.

You want to know why the dot-coms came crashing down? It's because many of them, not all, but many of them never had a way of ever making money. You see, one of the biggest fallacies of cyberspace is that it's cheaper to do business over the Internet than with the traditional brick-and-mortar approach. The logic is you don't have to build, lease, maintain, and staff expensive buildings. Makes sense right? In place of all those buildings just create a Web site.

The proponents of this theory forgot two important things. No, wait, they forgot a bazillion important things but these two particular items will do: *If you don't have a building how will anyone know you exist? And, better yet, how will you get the product to your customer?*

Let me see, if I have one of those expensive buildings, let's say in a well traveled mall, I not only have potential customers constantly coming by, but customers can see, sample and even walk away with my product. Instant gratification, delivery, and the ability to leverage the impulse buy. Not a bad trade-off for an expensive building.

A good example of these key points can be found in the case of Amazon.com and Barnes & Noble. When was the last time you saw a television commercial for a bookstore? My guess is never. Why? They don't need to spend money on expensive media. Their primary marketing strategy is location. Most major bookstores are located in malls or highly trafficked thoroughfares. They conduct some local newspaper advertising to promote book signings, coupon discounts and the like, but you won't see them spending huge amounts of money on promotions. They don't have to because those *outdated* buildings serve that purpose, among a number of others. Score one for brick-and-mortar.

Since being founded over 6 years ago, Amazon.com has not turned an annual profit. The general rule of thumb is a company should reach profitability within 5 years. Amazon did set a goal to be profitable on a pro forma basis in the fourth quarter of 2001, and they achieved that goal. You know pro forma? That's the accounting equivalent of now you see it now you don't. We made money, oops, no we didn't. Amazon actually posted a legitimate profit in Q4 2001, thanks to foreign currency gains.

The primary reason Amazon have never been profitable on an annual basis, is that initially they had to spend so much on marketing to hump their service and attract customers they couldn't be profitable. This has changed over the years. Amazon is now very well known. Too bad all the marketing money they no longer have to spend was replaced by the need to build a massive and complex distribution infrastructure.

Imagine that, a cyber business having to resort to constructing buildings to conduct business. That's the other part of the equation. I don't care how you do business you still have to get the product to the customer. Last time I checked, there were only two ways to do that; either you maintain inventory and deliver it yourself, or you pay someone to do it for you. Brick-and-mortar companies understood that even if they didn't quite understand the Internet. So Amazon spent a mountain of cash to build a distribution system capable of getting product to their customers in a timely and cost-effective manner. Score two for brick-and-mortar.

In contrast, Barnes & Noble turned a profit in every year from 1996 to 1999. They did lose money in 2000 though. Lamentably, for the dot-comers, that loss was due to Barnes & Noble's ownership position in Barnes & Noble.com. The brick-and-mortar side of the business actually made about $52 million. Damn, the curse of the dot-coms strikes again.

Getting back to our comparison, if it's cheaper to do business over the Internet then it would follow that Internet companies could pass on a better price to their customers and at least compete effectively on that basis. Well, even if you believe the total cost of sales is lower, you still have a little thing called shipping and handling.

In fairness, you could argue the cost of S&H is offset by the cost of getting to the bookstore. But that only holds true if you assume people make trips exclusively to go to the bookstore. I'm speculating here, but I suspect many of these trips serve multiple purposes. Thus the cost of the trip is amortized across a number of tasks. Even if someone does go just to a bookstore, it's probably because they want something immediately, not tomorrow, or next week. I'll be generous and call this one a wash.

Last item: *services*. Before you think I'm a dot-com basher, Amazon has done some very nice things in the area of personalized services. This is an advantage Internet businesses have over traditional brick-and-mortar. They can track every transaction. This allows them to tailor the screen (storefront) to the individual. They can also use the demographic information collected from their customers to up-sell and cross-sell. This is not only an opportunity to generate incremental revenue for Amazon, but it's a nice service to the customer.

Even on this point the tried and true brick-and-mortar businesses are not defenseless. True, they have no easy way to collect all those great customer demographics. There are things they can do to offer some semblance of personalization such as buyers clubs and e-mail newsletter services. I'm not an expert on the book business but I assume they are doing these and other things to gather better information about their customers.

But the brick-and-mortar guys are not sitting around twiddling their thumbs. Long ago the big bookstores did something clever from a marketing perspective. They found a way to expand their product base and simultaneously offer their own brand of personalized services. They expanded beyond books to sell music, magazines, and even coffee and donuts.

In place of being able to notify a customer the latest crime novel has arrived, they provide a *total buying experience* no cyber company can match. These days, buying a book is a great deal more than just a trip to the store. Many people enjoy browsing, seeing what bargain books may be available, checking out a CD or two, or having a Danish and cup of overpriced coffee. They may even read a magazine without having to buy it. Sorry Internet, you almost had one but I call this a wash too.

Let's see. What's the score? Brick-and-mortar two, dot-com zip. Three zip if you count the fact Barnes & Noble makes money. Making money should be good for at least a point, don't you think? The only way the dot-coms get on the scoreboard is if you count ties like they do in hockey. I don't follow hockey so ties count for zilch in my book.

When you get right down to it and analyze the realities of each business model, you see the Internet did not have the significant advantage it was touted to have over brick-and-mortar. Like almost everything, there are trade-offs for doing business purely electronically. Some advantages, yes, but many disadvantages as well. Those were blissfully ignored. If nothing else, we learned there is much more to building a successful business than just slapping up a Web site.

The primary reason for the utter collapse of the dot-com market was as basic as it gets. For some unexplained reason, people forgot the goal of a company is to make money. It's not to generate revenue or attract as many customers as possible. Repeat after me: *it's to make money*. I'd rather own a million dollar business with a 10 percent after-tax profit than a billion dollar business that loses money. Hey, but that's me. The million-dollar business isn't going to do much for the ego of a big company CEO. It doesn't look terribly impressive on the resume either. It just makes money. What a shame.

Oh sure, I suppose everyone convinced themselves these companies would eventually make money. However, no one dug very deep to validate that belief. People didn't do their homework. They blindly assumed everything would turn out fine. Blinded mostly by outrageous stock prices and the promise of wildly successful initial public offerings (IPOs).

I vividly remember how absurd it got when the hype about the new economy was in full swing. Brokerage houses were running radio spots that went something like this: One guy says, "The dot-com I invested in just lost twice as much money as last quarter." His buddy responds with chagrin. Then the first guy says, "It's great, the stock's up 50 percent!"

Here we had the investment community contributing to the

tragic misconception that losing money was a good thing. And you know, people bought it. They thought losing money was a good thing as long as you were increasing your page views and registered customer base. It was the old *I'll make it up in volume* strategy. Don't worry, when we get lots of customers we'll figure out how to be profitable. Sounds ridiculous now, doesn't it? News flash, it was ridiculous then too. People were just making too much money (at least on paper) to care.

So who is mostly to blame? In my opinion, the venture people. They can't pull a Pontius Pilate and wash their hands of this one, although many of them are doing their level best to try. They encouraged the poor little urchins running half these companies to concentrate on building a customer base and let cash flow be damned. Why? Because it didn't matter if you made money. You could IPO anything as long as you could show a high enough growth in your customer base. Don't worry, with all that capital from the stock offering you'll figure out a way to make money in the long run.

It was natural for the unsuspecting entrepreneur to go along with the program. They didn't know any better. Their investors and boards of directors were telling them to go full steam ahead and forget about profitability. And it was no small incentive that they also stood to make millions on their stock options. Why worry about what happens five or ten years down the road. We're in Internet time.

You remember Internet time? That was a classic. These guys must have known something no one else knew about Einstein's theory of relativity. You know what Internet time really was? It was a concoction to enhance the self-importance of the people involved. *I'm better than you because I can function in Internet time.* You ever hear the one about the tortoise and the hare? Now Internet time has a new meaning. In my book, it refers to the time it took those neophytes to go out of business. That's something they actually did accomplish faster than anyone else.

But there are no blameless people in the dot-com debacle, just different levels of blame. Everyone involved contributed to creating a great deal of pain and misery. All because they forgot, or chose to ignore, the most basic tenant in business. You have to be able to make money.

But if I were to allocate blame I'd put the VCs at the top. They could have stopped it from happening from the onset. How? Simple. Where were the business plans that demonstrated, at least on paper, how the businesses they invested in would eventually make money? Who was asking the tough questions to ensure there was a reasonable level of viability? That's the job of the venture capitalists. They are the first line of defense, so to speak. They not only failed to perform that function, they compounded their mistake and added fuel to the fire by giving horrible guidance.

Next in line: Wall Street. They went with the flow and hyped the market and profit potential, artificially inflating stock prices. No, they didn't start the fire. They just took advantage of the situation and by doing so fanned the flames. They failed to provide the normal market checks and balances that create legitimate stock valuations. We had businesses generating just a few million in revenue with multi-billion dollar valuations. Crazy now, but hindsight is perfect. The fact of the matter is it was crazy then and a lot of people on Wall Street knew it.

Last on the list are the little guys. If the average investor had stayed away from the feeding frenzy, perhaps much of what happened could have been avoided. Oh, but this is America. Present the average citizen who has some investment capital with a way to make a quick buck without working up a sweat and you won't be able to see the end of the line. No, the average citizen is also to blame. They may be last on the list and the group with the best excuses, but they are not without blame. We as a capitalistic society brought this on ourselves. The only good that can come from it is if we learned something.

This is all well and good, but why is the fact greed played a prominent role in the dot-com collapse relevant to every day business life? The dot-com disaster's significance is that it best illustrates how greed, when permitted to go unchecked, can wreak havoc.

Like it or not, greed is a fact of life – particularly in the business world. When properly applied it can be a positive influence. For instance, companies should be greedy about market share. They should always strive to gain more and more as long as they stay within the confines of the law. Companies should also be greedy about their desire to build revenue and profits. These are positive applications for greed.

But when greed turns personal, it crosses over to the dark side. The most frequent example of this occurs when the people who control companies put their personal wealth first. This invariably leads to decisions that artificially prop up the short-term valuation of a stock. You don't want to be with a company whose management team is exhibiting this kind of behavior. Eventually, the company will take a fall. Often it takes years to recover and it's not much fun to live through.

How can you recognize the signs? Listen to what management is saying. Are they unduly focused on the stock and its potential over the next year or two instead of what it might be worth over the next five years? Is there a pattern of decision-making that may help things temporarily but lead to problems down the road? In other words is there a lot of *robbing Peter to pay Paul* going on? If there is, eventually it will catch up with them because the impact tends to be cumulative. At some point the dam will burst.

The answers to these questions are sometimes hard to determine definitively. Most people are not privy to the same level of information as senior management. There can always be circumstances you may not be aware of which warrant their decisions. All you can do is monitor management's actions and make the best assessment possible given what you do know.

A more concrete way to understand what is motivating management is to watch what they do with their stock options. Senior managers selling stock options as soon as they vest is often a sign of a *take the money and run* attitude. Stock options usually vest over four or five years. When management teams are thinking long-term and truly acting in the best interest of the company, they tend to hold their options. They do so in the belief the stock will be worth more down the road. This is a good thing. You want to be with a company where this is the case.

On the other hand, if management sells their stock as fast as it vests, start looking for another job. Senior managers who misbehave in such a manner are probably just out to make a quick profit. They will be driven by getting the short-term stock price up even if it hurts the company down the road. They are probably spending as much time trying to find the next company to fleece as they are actually doing their job.

Another way to determine how senior managers operate is to research their history. Look at how long they stayed at companies and investigate their patterns of stock transactions. Also look at how well those companies did after they left. Usually, top managers who exhibit *carpetbagging* behavior are smart enough to get out before problems become public. Thus it is important to look beyond what the company did while they were there. What a company does 12 to 18 months after a manager leaves is the true sign of how well they did their job.

This is the lesson of the dot-com fiasco. Out of control greed can warp reality and impair judgment. In the case of the dot-coms it blinded us and made us believe making money didn't matter because a new economy was emerging.

There is no new economy. There never will be. There are only phases and advancements of the existing economy. Like an oil tanker, economies don't turn on a dime. Changes and progress take many years. Successful companies are built over decades. All businesses, whether brick-and-mortar or built in cyberspace, must adhere to one simple rule, now and a thousand years from now. They have to make money. Next time someone tells you a company's stock is going to double over night, ask them: Can the company make money?

CHAPTER THREE

As Luck Would Have It

Most of us are curious about what it takes to make it to the top of a profession. We wonder why some very capable people succeed while others do not. Successful people fascinate us. So much so we routinely turn them into celebrities without the slightest thought about how they got there.

This is not surprising. These days we make celebrities out of people who accomplish nothing more than excel at being devious. You need look no further than the latest craze of reality TV with shows like *Survivor*. One day Richard Hatch is an ordinary person and the next he's a radio talk show host. The funny thing is no one would have paid him a nickel for his opinion before Survivor. After he won, agents were no doubt lining up to represent him.

Watch out Imus here comes the H-Man, or more aptly the Hatchet-Man. Actually I should apologize to Imus. It is an injustice to mention his name and Richard Hatch' in the same sentence. Imus is a professional, with a track record of success, and well, Mr. Hatch' claim to fame is he pranced around an out of the way island in his birthday suit.

Thankfully, this type of fame is fleeting. Regardless, why does it happen at all? Richard Hatch wasn't a more enlightened person after Survivor. His opinion is no more valuable now than it was before. Yet, he and many others manage to capture our attention.

In the business world, Bill Gates is arguably the most fascinating person. We all know he achieved that status by founding and managing Microsoft into a world leader. So how did he do it? Is he that much smarter than everyone else? Is his celebrity status warranted simply because he was able to make a single company a success?

I'd like to share a story that illustrates the fine line between becoming Bill Gates and being virtually anonymous. I preface the story by saying I don't claim to have any firsthand knowledge of the events. I'm just relaying what I've gleaned from years in the industry and from what I've read, particularly in a book called *Gates* authored by Stephen Manes and Paul Andrews.

There are a number of lessons to be drawn from this story. Plus, it serves as an excellent example of a couple of common business mistakes such as the difficult decision to cannibalize an existing business and the failure to fully recognize the incremental revenue opportunities available from current customers. The failure to understand how to properly apply these concepts can severely impact a company's well being.

Further, the story illustrates the relationship between how we define luck and success. It's important to put luck in the proper context and to understand why *luck* is not simply a matter of chance.

It is also my hope that this story will serve to put success in the proper context. In my mind, believing successful people possess mystical talents is neither healthy nor necessarily correct. In some cases it may be true. Some highly successful people do possess skills far beyond the average person. However, most don't. They may be a little smarter than the average person, but magical they are not.

These people may be more like you than you think. There is no reason to put them on a pedestal. Perhaps you can learn something from them and perhaps you can't. Don't assume they have any deep insight. You may find yourself competing against them one day. If you do, the last thing you want to think is you can't win because they are too good at what they do. Nobody is unbeatable. That's the attitude you need to have, otherwise you've lost before you've started. What better way to illustrate this point than to show that even Bill Gates caught more than a few breaks along the way.

Lastly, the tale highlights two essential traits of achieving a high level of success and sustaining a market leading position. Traits you should look for in the CEO and management team of the company you work for. Traits you should try to cultivate in your own business personality.

The Microsoft story was made into a movie and numerous books have been written on the subject. The story is not new but I'm approaching it from a slightly different perspective. I won't be providing an historical account of how Microsoft and Bill Gates became Microsoft and Bill Gates. The perspective I give you will illustrate the subtle differences between fame and obscurity.

Once upon a time the PC didn't exist. I know, hard to believe for many gen X-, Y- and Z-ers. Then along came IBM who recognized the market opportunity. Oh, there were crude iterations of PC-like products before IBM, but it was Big Blue who hit upon just the right mix of features to spur the industry.

Though the market was wide open, time was still of the essence as other well established companies were also showing interest. To expedite getting to market, IBM formed a task force and commenced to quickly develop a product.

IBM's strength was hardware. Their core business was selling large, expensive mainframe computers…million dollar machines. Competitive pressure had forced IBM to move downstream to smaller computers, but nothing like the PC. Then, someone recognized the opportunity to create a device that would sell for thousands of dollars instead of tens or hundreds of thousands of dollars. More importantly, the device would be *programmable* and have an open architecture allowing third parties to create hardware add-ons and software applications, an innovative yet still controversial idea.

IBM realized from past experiences a closed architecture would inhibit the market. They also knew an open architecture would provide a competitive advantage. Despite all this, the decision to "open up" the PC was a radical one for IBM. By and large, computing technology was still proprietary and vendors maintained control over their platforms. This decision was paramount to the success of the PC and dramatically influenced the industry's direction.

For IBM, developing the hardware for the original PC was easy. That was, after all, their business. The task was made even simpler by the time-to-market constraints. The desire to get to market quickly required the initial product use mostly *off-the-shelf* parts. The challenge wasn't the hardware but getting the necessary software to make the hardware do something.

They needed three different types of software. They of course needed applications: spreadsheets and word processors and the like. However, before applications could be developed they needed the other two software components. One of these was programming languages to allow software developers to create the applications. The other and most critical was an operating system (OS). The OS is the basic set of software instructions defining the *ground rules* for all the application software. Every computing device has to have one.

IBM struggled mightily with the software. They attempted, unsuccessfully, to develop their own BASIC, an emerging programming language. The development costs soon exceeded the cost of acquiring the software. IBM raised the white flag and set out to license what they needed. At the time, Microsoft had already established itself as a leading supplier of programming languages, the most important of which was BASIC. So it was logical for IBM to turn to Microsoft. One problem solved.

Next, IBM needed an OS. Logic dictated they follow a similar path and seek out one of the leading OS companies. Given the PC market was a nascent market there weren't many choices. But hell, you only needed one. And one existed. A company called Digital Research (DRI) had developed an operating system called CP/M – Control Program for Microcomputers. The company was sort of a big fish in the little pond of the emerging PC world. As such, they were a logical choice for IBM to contact.

There was one minor catch. IBM had chosen a 16-bit processor for the PC and needed the 16-bit version of CP/M called CP/M-86. DRI hadn't finished the development effort on CP/M-86 and was not quite sure when they would. All in all, this should have been a minor problem.

Here is where the story gets good. Believe it or not Bill Gates was acting as a facilitator in this process. Gates, and Digital Research's founder, Gary Kildall knew each other well and assisted each other from time to time. The companies had a symbiotic relationship. Microsoft focused on programming languages while DRI's primary source of revenue was an operating system. Each benefited from the other's existence without being competitive.

At the request of IBM, Gates called Kildall to inform him IBM wanted to meet with the folks at DRI. But when IBM got there, Kildall was nowhere to be found. He had flown to the bay area on business. Whether or not that particular trip was critical is debatable. Kildall loved to fly and he had absolutely no respect for IBM or any big computer company for that matter. He felt they just screwed things up, so to hell with them.

Kildall was also a technical guy and didn't care much for business. If IBM needed technical expertise there would be plenty of people at the office to fill the void. Understanding the importance of protocol and diplomacy clearly was not Kildall's strong suit.

As it turned out, being stood up by Kildall was the least of IBM's problems. Cultural differences existed that made it difficult for the companies to get on the same page. For insight on how different DRI and IBM were, you need go no further than Digital Research's original corporate name. The company was initially called Intergalactic Digital Research. This speaks volumes about the mindset of the founders, not to mention the industry at that time. Imagine naming your company intergalactic anything. I'm hoping drugs were involved. At least they would have an excuse.

These cultural differences led to a general lack of trust and prevented the meeting from getting off the ground. The companies could not even agree on what is usually a mere formality, signing the perfunctory non-disclosure agreement (NDA).

For the uninitiated, NDAs are documents routinely signed by companies who plan to share confidential information. Most of the terms are generally industry standard; however NDAs from big companies like IBM tend to be a bit one sided. DRI objected to the wording of IBM's NDA and refused to sign. The meeting was over before it started.

Mind you, Gates had signed the exact same NDA just the day before. Signing an NDA doesn't obligate you to discuss confidential information. It just prevents the parties from divulging any of the confidential information they may receive. DRI should have just signed the thing to get the meeting rolling. They could have been cautious about what they discussed until they felt comfortable with the situation. They didn't do that. Instead, they wasted the entire day haggling over technicalities.

The turn of events stunned IBM who again asked Gates to assist. Jack Sams, the head of the software effort for IBM did finally talk with Kildall, but they never came to terms on pricing or a delivery date. They also never resolved the NDA issue.

Despite all the fits and starts in the initial meetings, the biggest problem DRI had was the fact CP/M-86 was late. If it had been ready on time it's likely IBM would have licensed it despite all the problems. If that happened Microsoft would never had gotten into the operating system business and likely would have never achieved their current status.

Kildall was myopic in his view and that led to some unforgivable tactical mistakes. *He failed to understand the value of a relationship with IBM.* True, the deal wasn't as attractive to DRI as it was to Microsoft. Microsoft could sell IBM an OS and still generate revenues from its programming languages. All DRI really had to sell was the OS.

Kildall felt if he licensed away the rights to his OS for a one-time fee he might be out of business. As I said, Kildall was a technical guy. Obviously he didn't have much of a head for business. Kildall could be the poster boy for sheer business stupidity. What the hell was he thinking? How many little companies do you know would thumb their nose at the proverbial golden goose? That is exactly what DRI did.

Look at it logically. Let's say DRI was on solid ground in viewing IBM as a threat to their existing business. *This is a common mistake companies make. They are so afraid to cannibalize their existing business they simply avoid doing so.* Now, on rare occasions that's the right decision, but most often it's a bad decision.

The reason is straightforward. If there is money to be made by cannibalizing an existing business and you don't do it, somebody else will. Companies don't operate in a vacuum. It's called free enterprise, and that's what this great nation was founded on. If there is money to be made someone is going to take a shot.

What did Kildall think was going to happen to his existing business when IBM started marketing a competitive product? Did he really believe IBM's entrance into the market would have no affect on DRI? I guess the answer to that question was yes.

It is shocking how often this mistake is made. The main reason is companies aren't willing to deal with the short-term pain such a transition can cause. The fact that, down the road, there may be a significant upside is often immaterial. Corporations find it difficult to place the proper weight on potential benefits that may be several years out.

This is a typical corporate mindset. Many management teams can't see beyond their noses, or in the case of public companies, beyond the next quarter. Even worse, some figure they can take the money and run before the proverbial shit hits the fan. Shameful but true.

But let's give Mr. Kildall the benefit of the doubt. Let's say his business would have been hurt. Think it through. IBM was the most powerful computer company in the world. There was some reason to be leery since IBM could dominate this fledgling market. If IBM were successful, maybe all of DRI's existing business would go away.

So what! If that happened wouldn't DRI be able to replace its existing business with all the new business generated by IBM? And wouldn't it have been logical to assume IBM's power and resources could take the business farther than any other company could possibly hope to? At a minimum, DRI could make money upgrading the operating system for IBM and other PC manufacturers. They could also develop enhanced versions of the OS and sell it themselves.

With IBM seeding the market, the potential installed base would be significantly larger than before. So worrying about what a deal with IBM would have done to any existing business was just dumb. In the long run, they would have been no worse off. They might have lost some control, but ultimately there would have been many more opportunities to make money.

The other mistake Kildall made was assuming he had to give CP/M away for a one-time fee. If you're so afraid of losing your business that you are prepared to walk away from the most powerful company in your industry, how could it hurt to put a counteroffer on the table? It doesn't even matter if you think they might refuse. Regardless of the potential impact to any existing business, there is usually a price that can make it worthwhile. That price may be totally unrealistic but there is no downside to asking. DRI never put an offer on the table. That, my friends, was moronic.

DRI had leverage. They already had the software. IBM obviously wanted to license it versus build it or they would not have bothered to have the meeting in the first place. Kildall also had to suspect Microsoft was talking with IBM regarding their development languages. Didn't he bother to feel Gates out as to what was going on? It's possible Gates would have provided some insight without breaking any confidentiality with IBM.

Not to mention IBM didn't need to steal anything from DRI. That was nothing more than paranoia. If they had bothered to sign the damn NDA they would have realized IBM was on a tight schedule and needed a partner to hit their launch dates. If DRI didn't have the software ready they should have just lied and figured out how to make it happen afterward. That's what Microsoft did. And they did it so well.

Oh, but that's not the end. It gets better.

Back at the ranch, Microsoft was continuing their discussions with IBM to license four programming languages. In late August of that year IBM and Microsoft signed a preliminary agreement that paid Microsoft to develop a software specification for the as yet unannounced PC. To do this, IBM needed to disclose the exact characteristics of the PC. This was the first time Microsoft knew what the product actually looked like.

Microsoft finally became aware of IBM's need for a 16-bit OS. With the relationship beginning to blossom, IBM consulted with Gates to see if he knew of any options. Microsoft actually had a 16-bit OS at the time but it wouldn't run on a low-end machine like the one proposed by IBM.

Never fear, Paul Allen, Gates' partner, rode to the rescue. Allen knew someone who might have what they were looking for. Tim Paterson, an employee of a tiny hardware company called Seattle Computer Products.

Paterson had also become frustrated waiting for Digital Research to finish CP/M-86. They had a similar problem as IBM. They needed CP/M-86 for a new product they had developed. Having tired of waiting, Paterson created a *clone* of CP/M-86 dubbed QDOS, the Quick and Dirty Operating System, later renamed 86-DOS. You have to love these early pioneers. They were a clever and industrious bunch.

But Seattle Computer still had a problem. They also needed programming languages so applications could be written for their hardware. To solve the problem Rod Brock, the man in charge of Seattle Computer contacted Paul Allen to propose a cross-licensing agreement. Microsoft could have the rights to 86-DOS in exchange for licensing rights to Microsoft's languages. This, as it turned out, was the seminal moment for Microsoft.

Microsoft was on the hook to deliver a proposal to IBM by the end of September. Jack Sams, who just happened to have a son the same age as Gates had taken Gates under his wing. The relationship had expanded beyond mere business partners and Sams was giving Gates advice on how to work with IBM. Inside knowledge that would prove beneficial. With IBM still getting nowhere with Digital Research, Sams suggested Microsoft include a 16-bit OS in their proposal.

Microsoft had already "over promised" a bunch of things to

IBM. Now they were faced with the prospect of promising an operating system they didn't have. This of course did not deter Gates. It was just one more detail, and ultimately, Gates realized, it would give Microsoft a great deal of control.

Allen called Brock to inform him they had a customer interested in sublicensing 86-DOS but couldn't reveal who because of confidentiality. Thank you NDA. The following day the two men reached a verbal agreement. By coincidence, this was the same day Microsoft submitted their preliminary proposal to IBM that just happened to include an operating system.

Paul Allen negotiated the rights to distribute 86-DOS. Microsoft could fully sublicense 86-DOS to another company for a $25,000 fee per company. It was a non-exclusive deal. Seattle Computer retained the rights to continue to market the product against Microsoft. But as a hardware company, marketing an operating system wasn't in their plans. To top it off, the poor schmucks at Seattle Computer agreed to continue to improve the product for Microsoft.

This was beautiful. Microsoft had acquired the rights to an operating system that they already had the largest computer company in the world on the hook to license. They got the company that actually developed the product to improve it, and they didn't even have to sign a contract for 60 days. If the deal with IBM fell through, Microsoft was out nothing. Even if IBM dropped out later on, Microsoft's total exposure was negligible. If negotiating were an Olympic event this deal would have won the gold, the silver, and the bronze.

Microsoft and IBM were scheduled to meet at the end of September. Meanwhile, Sams continued to coach Microsoft as to what should go into the final proposal. Not that Microsoft needed much help at this point. Gates already had support at the highest levels of IBM. Turns out, IBM's president John Opel was already aware of Microsoft. You see, Opel knew Mary Gates, Bill's mother, from the board of the United Way. Never hurts to have friends, or better yet mothers, in high places. Oh the network of the rich and powerful.

The companies didn't get a deal done in September but it wasn't because of IBM. It was most likely because Microsoft threw IBM a curve. They upped the ante on the license fee. IBM planned to use the software on a bunch of machines and Microsoft decided a one-time license fee or *flat fee* was no longer appropriate. Microsoft wanted royalties. Earth to Kildall, this is how business is done.

No question this was a ballsy move. It certainly wasn't typical at the time, especially between a small company and a big company. But as I said before, it never hurts to ask. Gates figured there wasn't any danger of screwing up the deal with an unreasonable offer. The worst that would happen was IBM would balk. If that happened, Microsoft could just back off.

Want to hear the best part? There's no suspense since we know the deal got done. But it was the timing and terms that were the icing on the cake. Microsoft is believed to have received an advance against royalties of $400,000 for the combination of DOS and BASIC. This was against a royalty of a buck for each copy. The royalty was moot though. Under the agreement if IBM included BASIC in ROM (Read Only Memory) on every PC no royalty would be paid. IBM of course included BASIC in every PC to avoid the royalty.

I doubt this bothered Gates much since be probably anticipated the move. Gates couldn't lose either way. By asking for the royalty Gates got something just as valuable. The loss of the royalty was more than offset by the benefit of having his version of BASIC included with each PC IBM sold. This gave Microsoft the upper hand in the development language business and helped fuel the early stages of the company.

The net result: Microsoft got hundreds of thousands of dollars for a product they didn't even develop. A product that only cost them $25,000 to acquire. What a deal.

Not to be outdone by Ron Popeil, "But wait, there's more!", the deal with IBM was signed in November. Microsoft still did not have an official contract with Seattle Computer. It wasn't until the day after Microsoft closed the deal with IBM that Seattle Computer even sent their formal proposal to Microsoft. As with most deals, they take longer than anyone expects and this one didn't get closed until early January. Microsoft had not only made an instant six figure profit, but they did it with a product they didn't yet formally have the rights to. How great was that!

You gotta love it. Bill Gates has a pair of platinum *cajones*. This is what separates him from the crowd. He is as aggressive and competitive as anyone in business. And when it comes to the killer instinct, he knows no bounds.

It's not that he's so much smarter than everyone else. Initially he was said to have viewed DOS as nothing more than a way to sell languages. He was in the process of making the same mistake the hardware guys made. Fortunately he got a wake up call early when a big distributor called Lifeboat Associates offered Microsoft a boat load (I couldn't resist) of money to resell DOS. This was the beginning of the cash cow that ultimately fueled Microsoft's application software business and their future dominance.

There is no denying a series of fortuitous events led to Microsoft becoming Microsoft. They certainly did not have the inside track and a number of companies had to make some large blunders to clear the way.

First, IBM did not understand the full opportunity before them. They failed to recognize one of the greatest if not the greatest *add-on* sales opportunities ever created. Think about it.

Once you seed the market and build an installed base of customers, what is one of the most basic things companies should try to do? Answer: sell into their base.

It's the easiest sale to make, although most companies do a poor job of it. Word of advice: you obviously want to grow your base, but you should never ignore add-on, cross-sell, or up-sell opportunities within your base. Logically, *incumbents* have a competitive advantage. They know the customer and the customer knows them. This is why it's the easiest and least expensive sale to make. It costs more to cultivate new customers than to sell additional products to existing ones. Growing and selling into the base should always be parallel efforts.

IBM didn't see the mother load of installed base selling: SOFTWARE! An almost endless supply of add-ons, as it were. A company could not have scripted a better scenario. And the *piece de resistance* was the operating system. Anyone who controlled the operating system would have a significant advantage in developing application software, not to mention the revenue from selling a copy of the OS with every PC.

Further, IBM should have realized from their mainframe experience, operating systems constantly evolve and improve. And what does that lead to boys and girls? Upgrades. That's the fuel that has powered the Microsoft empire. The proverbial cash cow. Too bad for IBM they had a hardware mentality.

It's one thing not to want to develop the operating system, it's entirely another not to want to control it. IBM could have easily negotiated control. They had all the cards. If Microsoft declined they could have found someone else. Hell, maybe Kildall would have finally seen the light. In all likelihood IBM was overly focused on the short-term time to market issues to worry about the long-term.

Ironically, both IBM and DRI made the same huge mistake. If

DRI had taken a more long-term view, DRI could have been Microsoft. Unfortunately for them, their judgment was clouded by the potential impact on their existing business. Bill Gates had the advantage of not having any existing operating system business to worry about. Nevertheless, Gates saw the potential and knew what was at stake. For that you have to give him a great deal of credit.

Even so, without his aggressive style none of this may have happened. This is what separates Gates from the crowd. He has no fear. He will never lay back and let another company get the upper hand. At times, Microsoft may be beaten but it's not because of passivity. Gates is willing to constantly *push the envelope* and he is supremely confident in his ability to perform under pressure. This allowed him to promise things most companies would never think of.

Add to this his killer instinct and more often than not he will win. Not because he's so much smarter or doesn't make mistakes, but because he constantly keeps the pressure on and is not afraid to act. These are the qualities topnotch management teams and entrepreneurs possess.

Gates may be the best but he is not alone. In the high tech industry people like Larry Ellison, the founder of Oracle, and Scott McNealy, the founder of Sun Microsystems share these qualities. The celebrated Jack Welch and Donald Trump also share many if not all of these traits. These are the characteristics you should seek in companies and, in particular, the CEO. If the CEO possesses these traits, the rest of the company will invariably follow suit.

These qualities by themselves do not guarantee success but they do greatly increase the probability of success. In the case of Microsoft, Gates' aggressiveness was an essential element to their ultimate success. However, none of it would have mattered if the two companies who had first crack had not erred. That's the thin line between being one of the richest men in the world and being one of a thousand other CEOs.

This chapter is titled *As Luck Would Have It* and to a degree it implies success or failure is a matter of luck. But luck alone is rarely the sole reason for success.

Webster's defines luck as: that which happens to a person, as if by chance, in the course of events; good fortune; advantage or success considered as the result of chance.

Was there chance involved with the creation of Microsoft? To a degree. There is chance involved in every action. Was Bill Gates lucky and the rest just unlucky? In part, but mostly Bill Gates possessed the necessary mindset and the rest didn't.

You know what luck really is? It's putting oneself in a position to take advantage of opportunities when they present themselves. You've heard the sayings, *being in the right place at the right time* and *when opportunity knocks*. These are only partly due to chance. Just as much if not more, they are due to being shrewd, knowing where opportunities may arise, and being equipped with the tools to leverage those opportunities. In other words, you make your own luck by being prepared and being on the lookout for opportunities.

That is exactly what Bill Gates did. Sure, a certain combination of events had to occur for him to be presented with the opportunity. But once presented, he knew what to do and was prepared to do it. That is precisely why, to many, successful people appear to be lucky. It's no coincidence that success and luck go hand in hand.

So Bill Gates is a billionaire. Gary Kildall, who died in 1994, and the founders of Seattle Computer are nothing more than footnotes in the history of the PC industry. A fine line indeed.

CHAPTER FOUR

The Price of Politics

Say a prayer for the dearly departed. During the writing of this book the videoconferencing company previously mentioned was acquired. The acquiring company was its primary competitor, a company who hadn't entered the business until the mid-'90s. The acquisition marked the beginning of the end for what was once the dominant company in the market. Like *The Blob* in the classic B horror movie, they will soon be integrated within the acquiring company's infrastructure. Slowly, their identity will fade, and ten years from now, no one will remember they existed.

This company once held over 60 percent of the market and had revenues of $450 million. At their peak, they had a market capitalization of over $1.5 billion. They once had the opportunity to be one of the more prominent companies in the world. Because someday, and you can certainly argue when, all of us will communicate visually. The idea of the Dick Tracy video watch will become a reality. Every computer, phone, and TV for that matter, will eventually become a device capable of real-time two-way visual communication.

This company could have been the driving force in making that happen. Instead, they limped to the finish line, being sold for what amounts to a few pieces of gold. A meager $362 million is all the company could command for a price. This was a better fate than going bankrupt. They had not turned a profit in years and were running out of cash. Nonetheless, in corporate terms, it was a fire sale.

Though there is no love lost, I was sad to see this happen. It didn't have to end this way. The company could have easily achieved long-term success, contributing valuable technology and improving the quality of life for many people. No longer. Now, the acquiring company has the opportunity to fill the void if they don't arrogantly squander it.

It's not the faceless corporate entity I'm saddened for. It's all the people. The years of talent and energy they committed to making the company a success were virtually wasted by a handful of greedy, misguided and self-serving individuals. I think about the lost productivity and the needless consumption of precious resources. And I think about how this happens all too often.

Bad karma? I don't know, but this will be the sixth company I've worked with that *disappeared* from the corporate landscape. Being involved in a volatile industry such as high tech may partially explain this fact. Technologies tend to come and go. You might even think that I just don't know how to pick companies. Here's an eye opener. Of the six deceased companies, five of them at one time were market leaders. And not in markets that have disappeared.

Six wasted opportunities. Six instances of resources devoured with little to show for it. Thousands of lives impacted, often by a few marginally or totally incompetent decision makers. Maybe I have seen more than my share of failed companies, or maybe it happens every day.

In an attempt to determine how widespread this problem may be, I decided to do a little research. Mind you, nothing scientific. But in reviewing a couple of Web sites including BankruptcyData.Com and ABI World, some interesting statistics came to light.

For example, would you like to hazard a guess on how many businesses filed for bankruptcy protection between 1980 and 2000? A whopping 1,263,321. That's a yearly average of 60,158. The annual average has been on the decline. In the '80s the annual average was 64,851 versus 57,934 in the '90s. This makes sense given the economic run we experienced in the '90s.

However, you might also expect filings to have continually declined during the '90s. That didn't occur. In the '90s bankruptcy filings actually increased four out of ten years and was relatively flat in three other years. In the decade of the '80s filings increased annually six times.

These statistics represent bankruptcy filings. It should not be assumed all these companies actually failed. Many may have returned to profitability after filing Chapter 11. Still, it's not a good thing to file for bankruptcy whether a company survives or not.

In fact, the only circumstance I know of where it pays to fail is major league baseball. In baseball the reward for owning a team that can't cut it is $250 million. To earn the honor of receiving a cool quarter billion, ordinary business failure just won't do. You have to be a *major league* screw up. I'm in the wrong business. I need to find one where you get paid to fail. It's a hell of a lot easier than being successful.

These statistics also don't provide insight regarding the size or type of companies. The vast majority of these were private companies and it's possible and probable many were small and under capitalized. Many likely failed for no other reason than a lack of financial resources. The numbers by themselves do not necessarily indicate widespread managerial problems. But you have to assume some percentage of the million plus companies failed because of politics or poor management. Even if that number is just 2 percent, that would be over 24,000 companies since 1980. I suspect the number is actually much higher.

If we examine publicly traded companies, more eye opening stats were uncovered. In 2000, a total of 176 publicly traded companies filed for bankruptcy with total assets of $94.8 billion. Of these companies, 21 had assets over $1 billion. In 2001 these numbers skyrocketed to a total of 257 filings. This is an almost 50 percent increase over the previous year. Further, the total assets of filings in 2001 ballooned to $258.5 billion and the number of billion dollar companies filing more than doubled to a total of 45. This is a very disturbing trend.

Needless to say, the disruption caused by a billion dollar company going through Chapter 11 is enormous. No matter the outcome, thousands of jobs are lost and tens of thousands of lives are impacted. And lest you think these are obscure companies, the list of failures includes many household names. Polaroid *overexposed* itself financially, Vlasic found itself in a *pickle*, and Converse *sneaked* into insolvency. (Groan if you want to, I couldn't resist.) Other notables include TWA, Owens Corning, Levitz Furniture, Montgomery Ward, Schwinn, Burlington Industries, and Sunbeam.

Sunbeam? The maker of Mr. Coffee™? Say it ain't so! Oh the humanity. How can a company who markets an American icon like Mr. Coffee go belly up? By cooking the books, that's how. Shame on them. Joe DiMaggio is probably rolling over in his grave. I'm just glad I don't drink coffee. I'd really be upset.

I better finish this book fast because two more prominent billion-dollar companies just went Chapter 11. The two new entries into the business hall of shame are Chiquita, who must have slipped on one too many banana peels, and Enron Corporation.

Enron, a once elite energy company proudly owned the naming rights to the Houston Astros ballpark. Now, they are the proud owner of the mother of all bankruptcies. With revenues of over $100 billion in 2000, Enron has the dubious distinction of being the biggest bankruptcy filing in history.

The entire Enron debacle has mushroomed into a huge media event. Every politician in the country is attempting to grab a piece of the spotlight to pontificate their indignation on how this could happen while simultaneously scrambling to give back all the money they accepted from this bunch of unethical, greedy, bastards. And a plethora of government agencies and committees are investigating not only Enron's management for criminal behavior, but their auditors, Arthur Andersen, as well.

These investigations are all well and good. If they find criminal behavior I hope they send the lot of them to jail. And I don't mean the Michael Milken summer vacation kind of jail. It's time for us to start treating so-called white-collar crime as a real crime. Given the harm these guys have done to thousands of people, if criminal conduct is found they should do hard time and a lot of it.

But even if that happens, it won't have addressed the root causes of the problem. As usual, we will have treated the symptoms and not the problem. Enron is my *poster company* for the primary message of this book. When the dust settles it will epitomize everything that has gone awry with our corporate system. The root causes of the Enron collapse can be found in a corporate culture designed to satisfy management's egos and Wall Street's insatiable need for rapid growth. Expect to hear much more from me about this entire affair.

The Enron failure has certainly brought attention to the human impact a company failure can have. But have you ever stopped to think how failures such as this impact our world?

Politics was largely to blame for the previously mentioned videoconferencing company's decline. Too much energy applied to individual self-serving acts. Too much time wasted putting off decisions because of uncertain political winds. Too much time protecting one's own butt. Most of the time this behavior just wastes time and money. But for this company it was nearly fatal. Despite being bailed out, indulging in politics cost the stockholders over $1 billion in lost value.

Ever wonder what the cost of politics is at a macro level? Or how much more productive we could be as a business community if we did not apply so much energy to political endeavors? Not even counting the companies that are mortally wounded by such behavior, I estimate, as an economy, we could instantly increase productivity by 10 to 15 percent by eliminating politics. In lean economic times, those savings could have a significant impact.

Why do I say 10 to 15 percent? Honestly, it's just a SWAG (scientific wild-ass guess). It's an intuitive estimate based upon experience. Factored in is the impact from delayed decisions caused by waiting to be certain of what management wants. That's a political act. Or the time and energy consumed by people who focus on self-promotion or sticking it to a colleague to gain a personal advantage. Those are clearly political acts. Also considered is the cost of bad decisions made simply to enhance one's own stature. That is the worst political act of all. I think I'm probably on safe ground with my estimate.

You may consider all of this Darwinian, and to a degree it is. I'm a great believer in Darwin. Survival is the right of the fittest, but there is a difference between natural evolution, as defined by Darwin, and *corporate evolution.*

The difference in the corporate world is we are not talking about species and their ability to evolve. We are talking about humans with the ability to think and reason. We have a unique advantage in our ability to assimilate information and invent what we need to survive. There is rarely a good reason for companies who achieve leadership status to fail. More often than not, the reason is a general lack of ability on the part of management.

Even if you make the age-old buggy whip argument, I would contend they too had an opportunity to be successful doing something else. When the car was invented, buggy whip manufacturers should have seen the handwriting on the wall. If they did, they could have transitioned to making driving gloves, seat covers, or similar products. Those who did would have likely survived, and those who didn't probably went out of business. But that was not a matter of fitness. It was a matter of being stupid.

Sure, in some cases there may have been an inability to transition. Insufficient capital or lack of skilled labor for example. These would be cases of Darwinian evolution. But my gut tells me most of them probably just refused to accept the inevitable.

One could also argue that when companies fail, other companies fill the void. In those companies, resources may be used more wisely and lives may be impacted for the better. Still, it does not make it any less a waste of time and energy.

As a species, we have a tendency to waste the opportunities afforded us after achieving positions of leadership. This is not just a problem in the business world but the political world as well. We continually fail to heed the lessons of history, and as the saying goes, those who forget history are doomed to repeat it.

Success can make people complacent. It alters priorities, and not in a positive way. It is why every great empire before us has failed - the Greeks, Romans, and British. Will America follow its predecessors or will we learn from history? Are we losing the edge that made us a great power? Are we overly consumed with personal wealth? Melodramatic? Maybe. Or perhaps I'm just a pessimist. Or maybe the signs are right in front of us and we refuse to acknowledge them. Something to think about.

A FINAL THOUGHT

The above words were penned prior to the disaster of September 11th. It is my hope that this unconscionable act of barbarism will cause our nation to reflect on how blessed we are to live in this country, and to realize that with these blessings comes a great responsibility. We are the mightiest power this planet has ever known, and that position in the world community should never be taken for granted.

Nothing will ever adequately compensate those who lost loved ones. But if our nation and humankind learn from this tragedy and react properly, those who made the ultimate sacrifice can be partially consoled by the knowledge their loss resulted in advancing society as a whole.

It cannot be stressed enough that we can no longer take things for granted. Not our security, and not our status as the only remaining economic and military superpower. Being the most powerful nation is not a birthright. We achieved it through hard work and determination. More importantly, our belief in democracy had made us the first dominant nation not to overtly inflict our will on the rest of the world. This, as much as anything, has allowed us to preserve our greatness. We must maintain that mindset.

Being the most successful democratic society in history carries with it an obligation to use our leadership position not only to increase our own wealth, comfort, and security, but also to assist in increasing the wealth, comfort, and security of every nation. Ultimately, this effort will improve the lives of citizens of all countries, including the United States. We will benefit by snuffing out the root causes of unrest and terrorism, and by creating new and stronger economic trading partners. To accomplish this will require a sustained application of all our military, economic, and political resources. Success will depend on replacing our desire for instant gratification with the determination to achieve the long-term goal.

We can only hope this wake up call and the unity the world showed in its aftermath is not short lived. We must also hope our leaders, and the leaders of other nations, possess the wisdom to balance the short-term goals of security with the long-term goals of advancing civilization as a whole. And most importantly, we, as individuals, must continue to apply the principles on which this country was founded in both our personal and business everyday lives.

Rest in peace.

PART TWO · THE HEART

CHAPTER FIVE

The Life Blood of Business

A lthough admittedly biased, it is difficult to argue with the premise marketing should be the primary driver for most businesses. As with all things there are exceptions. In some companies the benefits of marketing may be secondary. The importance of marketing also varies depending upon where a company is in its life cycle. Regardless, for the vast majority, sustainable long-term success is dependent upon recognizing marketing as the heart of business.

First, let's examine a possible exception. We'll use a fictitious company as an example. Let's say there is a company whose entire business is selling parts directly to car manufacturers. The company doesn't sell to consumers and its target market is small and well defined. Let's also say the company itself is relatively small and has been successful by focusing their expertise on building just a few products.

This situation dictates a higher priority be placed on the roles of engineering, quality control, and operations. The challenge for a company such as this is the timely delivery of quality parts.

Marketing can still play a role in anticipating potential customer needs, facilitating communications, and possibly developing ideas for synergistic new products. Marketing's value in this scenario may be diminished, but not eliminated.

It is also critical to understand that marketing's importance tends to grow as a company grows. In the early stages of a start-up, marketing is not normally the focus. The emphasis a start-up places on marketing is dependent upon the company's product. For instance, a service-based business might require marketing at an earlier stage than a product-based business.

However, in general, marketing should take a back seat to other functional areas in the early stages of a company's maturation.

Given my familiarity with technology, we'll use high tech as an example. Other industries undoubtedly have similar characteristics.

Inventive engineers are typically the catalyst for technology start-ups. Their technical skills allow them to recognize potential market opportunities and devise clever ways to apply technology to address those opportunities. In a technology company's initial stages, the focus is on product development.

Sure, someone has to evaluate the market and validate the business model, but those activities are usually conducted prior to raising money. For the sake of our example, we'll assume that work has been completed. Given this, the first year or so of the company's existence is usually dedicated to product development.

When the product approaches completion, operations and customer support become priorities. These functional areas lay the groundwork for the manufacture and support of the product. In small companies it's not unusual for engineering to double as customer support. However, if resources permit, the preference is to create a separate support capability to keep engineering focused on development issues.

Once these functions are in place, next to kick in is sales. The distribution strategy will dictate the exact sales requirements. The focus will differ for a direct sales model versus one that uses third party distribution channels. The sales strategy chosen is often predicated on the type of product and market. The point is a company needs to establish distribution before any marketing effort can pay dividends. The sales organization will drive the initial revenue stream.

As the company matures, marketing becomes increasingly

important. The time frame for marketing to elevate to the primary business driver is dependent upon individual circumstances. Every situation is unique and an array of variables comes into play. Determining the proper time is one of those business decisions where there is no substitute for experience.Product management is normally the first area of marketing to become important. This occurs sometime prior to shipping the initial product. Secondary are all the marketing communication functions such as public relations, advertising, and the creation of collateral. Everything in this second tier happens in phases, with the creation of collateral and public relations coming first. As the company progresses, the level of sophistication and frequency of these activities increases.

Once a company has shipped its first product and begins to develop follow-on products, product management begins to evolve from supporting the development effort to driving the development effort, and marketing needs to be in full swing. By this I mean marketing needs to analyze the market, determine on-going customer requirements, and identify new product opportunities. Simultaneously, the marketing communications function becomes more complex. The need to create advertising or direct mail campaigns may develop and so on and so forth. You get the picture.

The net of this is the role and importance of marketing will evolve as the company and market evolve. Ultimately, for almost every company larger than a mom and pop business, marketing should become the driving force. Although the timing will vary, the goal should be to become marketing-driven early on.

There are a host of reasons to support this position. For one, marketing, by definition, is chartered to analyze the market and determine customer requirements. Fundamentally, the success or failure of any company is predicated upon whether customers will buy their products. It's logical to assume the people responsible for figuring out what customers want should drive this process. Given this, marketing should guide product direction.

Additionally, marketing's mindset is ideally suited to chart a company's direction. Marketing is not unduly influenced by short-term requirements. A well-functioning marketing department is staffed with individuals who can balance short and long-term needs. Marketing looks beyond the next quarter or two and analyzes the business three to five years out. This puts them in the best position to drive a company's long-term success. I contend no other department within an organization possesses these necessary qualities.

Let's look at the alternatives.

A company can be engineering-driven. Many technology companies fit this mold. In engineering-driven environments, technical people, who often don't possess a full understanding of the market dynamics make the decisions. This is not a knock on engineers. Their skills are suited to product development not deciphering market dynamics.

With their technical background, engineers are prone to building products that are interesting to build rather than products that are useful to the market. There is a tendency for the technical mindset to design a Cadillac when the market only needs a Chevy. This phenomenon occurs because there is often a higher level of job satisfaction in building complex products rather than mundane commodity-like products.

Engineering is also prone to biases stemming from their level of expertise. Engineers have such a thorough understanding and appreciation of technology and its associated benefits, they can lose sight of the fact less technical people might not share their enthusiasm. Generally speaking, this is not a good thing.

It should be noted, at least in high tech, engineers are often successful in starting companies. But as often, they stumble when trying to grow them. The reason is a shift in market focus. As markets mature, products and technology take a back seat to marketing and distribution. In the early stages of a company the focus is on building and delivering the initial product. Initial products invariably break new ground either in what they do or how they do it. Companies gain a foothold because they have built a better mousetrap.

As time passes, other companies bring similar products to market and it becomes increasingly difficult to maintain any substantial product differentiation. Not that product differentiation ever becomes irrelevant, it never does. But as products migrate toward commodity status, other factors begin to play a more critical role.

Engineering-driven companies oft times overlook this shift and the true market requirements. This results in a decline in business. The landscape of the high tech industry is littered with the carcasses of such companies. The entire minicomputer industry is an example. DEC and Wang are the poster boys. Billion dollar companies that went up in smoke because they never made the transition from being engineering-driven to being marketing-driven.

All right, engineering doesn't seem to be a good candidate to drive a company. What about sales? Not that long ago corporate America had a sales-driven mentality. Interestingly, in the '70s, the distinction between marketing and sales was not well understood. It was common to have marketing departments staffed with ex-sales people and rarely did anyone achieve the level of VP of marketing without having some sales experience. My first marketing VP told me I would never become a VP of marketing if I didn't at some point go into sales. He was wrong, mostly because he was a sales guy and assumed the business mentality would never evolve.

Sales and marketing are two very different disciplines with two distinct mindsets. Marketing needs to see the big picture and have a long-term view. Sales must be single-minded, narrowly focused, and short-term oriented. Sales people are driven by immediate gratification. Their entire goal is to make the quota. Given this, sales people rarely look beyond the current quarter. They can't afford to. Their paycheck is dependent on making the number. Now.

Sales people are also prone to giving a customer whatever they ask for. They don't consider whether anyone else may want a specific feature or product nor do they think about what it might cost to build. Generally, they are driven by their accounts and getting the sale. That's their role. That's what they need to do to be successful. It just isn't a good mentality to lead a company.

Sales-driven companies will, more often than not, collapse. They frequently misuse resources and fail to recognize shifting market conditions. They may succeed for a while, but sustaining success is difficult.

OK, sales doesn't appear to be a good option. How about finance? This has potential. The goal of a company is to make money and who understands the dollars and cents aspect of business better than finance? True, finance understands the inner workings of accounting and the money aspects of the business better than anyone else. The problem is, their comprehension of business tends to end there.

Finance people are not all that different from technical people. Instead of designing and building things, they manipulate numbers on a balance sheet. The financial mindset is often mechanical in nature, highly focused, and overly conservative. Rarely do finance people possess a complete understanding of the story behind the numbers. The decisions they make are often driven purely by the goal of improving the current versus the future bottom line.

Improving the bottom line is absolutely a good thing. However, the way you go about achieving that goal varies. Finance people are inclined to be conservative because the more risk you can eliminate the more predictable the numbers become. This conservative mindset can limit growth. Financially-driven companies can potentially sustain their position for very long periods of time. The problem is they will either grow very slowly or not at all. If you like boring little companies, look for one that is finance-driven.

What does that leave? Manufacturing/operations, human resources, customer support? I don't think we need to go into detail about these disciplines. There are cases of companies being manufacturing-driven but these are companies in very specialized areas. I've never heard of a company being led by human resources or customer support, so that brings us back to marketing.

By its very definition one can understand why marketing is critical. The role of marketing is to access and analyze the market and identify opportunities for new and existing products. This is a fancy way of saying, figure out what customers want and build it. It's kind of hard to argue the primary driver for a company should be to build stuff that people want. It's marketing's job to figure out what that stuff is.

Determining what people want is not limited to just product features. It also means analyzing pricing and distribution strategies. For example, you may want a big screen TV but you wouldn't pay $10,000 for it. You may also prefer to buy it from a store versus ordering it mail order. You get the idea. Marketing needs to examine all the factors that influence a buying decision and devise a strategy that fits. They are the only department responsible for looking at all aspects of the business.

Top-notch marketing requires a range of skills and an all-encompassing long-term view. These skills need to be directed outward to assess the market as well as inward to facilitate the process.

The outward role of marketing involves continually assessing the market. This is not limited to an individual market either. It can include an entire industry and even the economy as a whole. This is due to the fact that forces external to a particular market can impact that market. We can use our big screen TV example again. Sales of luxury items like big screen TVs are affected by overall economic conditions. If the economy goes south, so will sales of expensive TVs. Marketing's responsibility is to be on guard and try to anticipate changing market forces.

Marketing is responsible for identifying, defining, and communicating to the target market. This involves interpreting market research, analyzing demographics, creating business plans, and developing promotional strategies. Aren't all these activities central to a company's success?

The inward focus of marketing requires it to be a multi-faceted discipline. It is the only functional area that requires an understanding of all other functional areas. What do I mean? In the course of doing business, marketing interacts with almost every department within an organization. I like to compare marketing with being the conductor of an orchestra. Just as a conductor is responsible for setting the direction of a musical score, marketing is responsible for setting the product direction and often the direction of the company as a whole.

For music to sound like music rather than noise, every section in an orchestra has to execute their part. The strings, brass, and percussion sections all have to play the right note at the right time. Business is no different. In business, engineering has to architect the right product and make it work. Manufacturing has to build it. And sales has to sell it. If any of these individual functions fail, the entire process is likely to fail.

Like a conductor, marketing has the responsibility of keeping everyone in unison. Marketing is responsible for defining products by determining what the market wants. They work with development to facilitate the creation of the product. They develop a distribution strategy and create the necessary sales tools to sell the product – the product positioning, competitive knock-offs, product presentations, and so on.

But before a product can be sold, it has to be built. To accomplish this, marketing works with sales, manufacturing, and finance to forecast the product. They interface with operations to ensure manufacturability in the timeframe and quantities required.

And it doesn't stop there. Marketing is responsible for ensuring product profitability. You can have a great product that doesn't make money and I think we covered the fact that is not good. So marketing works with finance to evaluate expected margins and return on investment. In an effort to avoid unacceptable levels of customer dissatisfaction marketing even liaises with the support organization to make sure training levels are adequate.

Unlike any other department, marketing is responsible for looking at the entire business landscape and providing the necessary guidance for all other functional areas to ensure overall success. A lot like the function of the heart.

I'm not suggesting every company needs a CEO who comes

from marketing. I think individuals with marketing backgrounds are well suited to become CEOs but the skills required to be a good CEO transcend marketing.

Financial oriented companies such as banks and investment firms are well served with leaders from financial backgrounds. Some highly technical companies may even be better off with a technical person at the helm. But regardless of the background of the person heading the company, I contend they need to let marketing lead the way.

Given this, everyone, no matter whether they pursue a career in engineering, finance, or sales, should have a basic understanding of the role and responsibility of marketing. For senior management, understanding the importance of marketing and fostering a marketing-driven culture is imperative. Again, I'm admittedly biased, but I believe the best and most successful companies will follow this path.

In building your career, developing a broader knowledge of the dynamics of marketing can provide a significant edge. It will help you to identify companies who truly have a marketing-driven culture versus those who merely pay lip service to marketing. And the deeper your knowledge, the better positioned you will be to recognize the signs of good and bad marketing. It's one thing to want to be marketing-driven, but you still need the skills to execute. One without the other doesn't do you much good.

Have I managed to make the case for marketing? I hope so. If not, I'm kinda screwed and I guess you are too. You plunked down some hard cash for this book. Cash I have no intention of giving back. And I've lost any opportunity to sell you another product. As a marketing person that pains me greatly. So I hope you start turning to the next page right now.

It Ain't Rocket Science But...

All right. If you're reading this page, it would seem the book didn't hit the trash. This is definitely a positive sign.

In developing any product, including this book, the ideal scenario is to create some unique characteristic. This is commonly referred to as the unique selling proposition or USP. It is also referred to as the *value proposition* and is a staple of marketing. Not that it's always possible, but it is always desirable, providing it's done right.

Being unique is not automatically beneficial. There is bad unique as well as good unique. To work, the unique characteristic has to be consistent with the overall positioning of the product and, ultimately, has to be useful to the consumer. Duh. That's not much of an intellectual revelation. Well, you'd be surprised how many features nobody cares about except the designers, get proposed, or worse, integrated into a product. Remember our Cadillac versus Chevy example? It happens quite often in high tech and although it sounds obvious, sometimes it isn't.

For instance, could a commercial, within a book of all places, possibly provide *good* uniqueness? We're about to find out. Commercials are intended to entice the target audience (uhh, that's you) to buy a product (uhh, that's this book); however in this case, the product is not entirely the book itself. True, the book is the physical representation of the product but the words comprise the *value* of the book. And that's where the commercial comes in.

Books, like movies, have an interesting aspect to them. These products have a significant personal element. Unlike most products that are branded by the companies who produce them, the branding of a book or movie stems more from the personality and/or capability of the creator or actor rather than from the personality of a corporate entity. You may buy a car from Ford because you feel good about the company, but you have no idea who actually created the car. Not so with books and movies.

Consumers buy books and go to movies because they expect to be entertained, or in the case of non-fiction, they expect to obtain useful information; however the reason for selecting a particular book or movie is often based on the writer, director, or actor.

That being the case, wouldn't it be important to accomplish a couple of things from a product standpoint? For one thing, as a writer, credibility needs to be developed. The reader has to believe the author has the capacity for rational thought and a sufficient background to offer valid comments on the subject. Without that credibility, a book is nothing more than a bunch of words on a page. Second, it may also be beneficial to develop a persona in the same way publicists do for entertainers. Sounds like a reasonable marketing strategy.

As you might assume from the previous chapter, the knowledge required to excel at marketing is extensive. A foundation in areas such as economics, statistics, psychology, and advertising, to name a few, is essential. Beyond that, marketing also needs an understanding of the basic elements of development, manufacturing, sales, finance, and support.

Making the entire process a bit trickier is the fact that unlike the conductor who has authority over the musicians, marketing has no direct authority over other departments. Marketing needs to orchestrate all the internal activities without ordering people around. People skills become very important, as do the proper level of verbal and written communication skills.

This being the case, the first quality on the list of things needed to excel in marketing is intelligence. Not unlike an IQ test, effective marketing in both the planning and execution stages involves a continual stream of problem solving. The process is in a constant state of flux and it's marketing's charter to continually assess the current status, make any necessary corrections, and execute those changes.

Caution! Shameless self-promoting commercial ahead...

How do I stack up against the intelligence benchmark?

For all you know I could simply be someone who has made some money meandering around the high tech industry acting like a marketing person. That doesn't mean I really *know* anything, or that I'm the least bit smart. A lot of people get pulled along for the ride. Why should you believe anything I say? Maybe some academic highlights would help.

I graduated second in my class in high school. I would have been first but I joined my classmates in a boycott of a chemistry test in my senior year. This resulted in a less than stellar grade knocking me down to the two spot when the eventual winner showed up for the test. Brown-noser!

I can't recall why we did it, a protest for something the teacher had done. My guess is the teacher was right and we were wrong. Hell, we were high school students. You're never wrong at that age. I wish they had told me there was a cash prize for being valedictorian, I probably would have been sitting right beside my brown nosing little classmate. I always had a mercenary streak.

I went on to graduate seventh in my class at Fordham University with a 3.83 grade point average and a degree in Computer Management. I then earned an MBA from Pepperdine University. Oh yes, I did both while holding down a full time job. Considering I never liked school and applied nothing more than a minimal effort, not a bad track record.

One last item: I once took a series of IQ tests just for the hell of it. I'll be honest. I don't remember the exact scores. I took several tests and admittedly the scores improved with practice. Then again, that is the desired result. The ability to learn and apply is the very definition of intelligence. Anyway, the point is my average for the series of tests was in the 140s. I think that's a pretty good number.

I mention all of this because these are recognized measures of intelligence. I don't personally put a great deal of credence in the value of an IQ test other than to measure, in its most basic form, the ability of the brain to figure things out. This is not insignificant, but it does not necessarily translate into any practical skill.

Corporate management is filled with intelligent people. There are very few truly stupid people in management. The problem is not a shortage of intelligent people but rather a shortage of people who can properly apply their intelligence on a consistent basis.

So do I have the ability to apply this intelligence? On this point my record is clear. The ability to quickly assess situations is a source of pride for me. Comprehending new products and markets within 90 days is a skill honed over many years. It is a skill particularly important for a consultant. In the consulting world there is no learning curve. You need to grasp issues quickly or find another vocation.

The most notable example of this came not long ago with a consulting assignment for a little company called AT&T. The deliverable was a comprehensive market analysis. AT&T wanted to know if there was a market for a technology platform they had developed for internal use. The catch was, I didn't even know the market in question existed prior to the assignment. Adding a further level of complexity was the fact the assignment was in telecommunications, an industry in which I possessed no particular experience.

I had 42 working days to deliver a report to one of the largest telecommunications companies on the planet and I didn't know anything at all about the market. Fortunately, there was an absolutely terrific technical expert who assisted. Without him, it would not have been possible to meet the deadline. But with his help, by the completion date, perhaps the definitive study on this particular market had been produced. The report was over 160 pages in length and under normal circumstances might have taken a team of professional researchers twice as long to produce.

The icing on the cake occurred when we presented our findings to a conference room filled with people who had spent their entire careers in telecommunications. At presentation's end, everyone was convinced I was an expert in the field. This was despite the fact I had a little over two calendar months worth of experience. I felt like *The Pretender*. Remember that TV show? Some intellectual freak goes around impersonating different types of people – doctors, fighter pilots, etc. Of course he's better looking and does more exotic stuff. I confine myself to applying that particular skill to the business world.

End of commercial. Oh, by the way, there's another commercial later on but I'm not going to tell you when. I want you to be surprised. (That's code for, *I don't want you to skip over it.*) Hey, I'm a marketing guy. It's my job.

CHAPTER SIX

Optimism Can be Hazardous to Your Health

Now there's a cheery thought. You're probably thinking what kind of wacko is this guy? I mean, how can anyone make a statement like that? It goes against every bit of feel good psychobabble spewed forth by the pop psychology guru *du jour*. How can anyone succeed in life without being optimistic? Let me explain a couple of things.

The problems caused by out of control optimism are related to the tendency to ignore the downside and the overwhelming desire to *please* management. My position is you don't need to be optimistic to succeed. You need to be (1) confident, (2) prepared, and (3) realistic. I believe that confidence and preparation, grounded in realism, is the correct approach.

Unfortunately, the value of realism is often lost in the world of business. An optimistic mindset can frequently escalate into the realm of fantasy. This was never better highlighted than by the last decade or so of the stock market, before reality brought it back down to earth. None other than Alan Greenspan, the chairman of the Federal Reserve, once uttered the term "irrational exuberance" when referring to the fact the stock market was increasing in value without any real economic foundation. This is a perfect example of optimism gone awry. People just believed stocks would continue to increase in value. Their optimism was unbounded and unfounded.

There are countless examples of realism being set aside in favor of optimism in the corporate environment. A classic and repetitive one comes from the market research community. If you've ever seen a typical market research company forecast for a new class of product you're familiar with the dreaded *hockey stick* curve. For those unfamiliar, a hockey stick curve is the name given to a product forecast whose characteristics include very low revenues in the first couple of years followed by explosive growth in the next few years. Picturing this curve in your mind, it looks like a hockey stick.

Market research firms are notorious for creating these types of forecasts. The reason is simple. Companies who pay for the research are often looking for third party confirmation of a market's ability to yield high growth. It's a case of telling them what they want to hear. Research firms wouldn't make much money if they tried to sell reality because it's not nearly as attractive.

The consequence is companies base business plans around these forecasts. Ever hear the phrase garbage in, garbage out? Garbage is what you get when you believe in these projections. In all my years in technology I've never seen one of these hockey stick forecasts actually come to fruition. I suppose it has happened, but it would be the exception to the rule.

There may be industries, such as the toy/gaming industry, where new products can experience meteoric growth – a product like Cabbage Patch dolls. To accomplish such growth requires a certain set of characteristics. For the most part, products have to be relatively low-cost. Also, the chances of rapid acceptance are much greater for products targeted directly toward consumers versus businesses. Lastly, a product hoping to experience quick growth cannot require behavioral changes by the user.

Technology, whether it's computer related or consumer electronics, doesn't tend to have the characteristics necessary for rapid growth. More often, new technology and consumer electronic products are initially expensive. HDTV is a good example. HDTV won't gain wide acceptance until it sells for about what standard TVs sell for today.

In the computer field, new technologies and products frequently require a behavioral change on the part of the user. Voice mail and e-mail illustrate this point. Although ubiquitous today, neither of these technologies was immediately embraced by the market. Behavioral changes are one of the biggest impediments to acceptance a product can face, regardless of its value.

It's been my experience, almost every new technology takes a minimum of seven years to reach critical mass. I can't say for certain the same is true for other industries, but I suspect similarities exist. It takes time for the market to absorb new products, no matter how good they are. People and companies just do not change overnight.

This estimate of seven years is by no means hard and fast. But it is a reasonable average. I also suspect this time will compress in the future as the general pace of society continues to increase.

So maybe it's not prudent to believe in *aggressive* forecasts. Still, optimism is generally a good thing. Don't you want to foster an environment where everyone feels positive and upbeat? I say, if that's what you're looking for go to an Amway meeting. You'll find an entire subculture of people who believe in the power of positive thinking. Or, if you're not into selling soap to all your friends and family, try a Tony Robbins seminar. It just gives me goose bumps thinking about all the happy can-do thoughts that happen in that contrived environment.

But let's get back to the real world. You remember that place, the one where shit happens. My approach is to replace optimism with three things: confidence, preparation, and realism. Give me one employee who is prepared and supremely confident in their ability to succeed and I guarantee they will kick the crap out of an entire team of optimistic thinkers who don't know which way is up when things go wrong.

Honestly, optimistic people have a tendency to get on my nerves. Yes, this is another blanket statement and it is clearly unfair to people who are optimistic by nature but also possess the genuine qualities necessary for success. I have to tell you, though, when it comes right down to it, I don't understand the whole concept of optimism.

Webster's definition of optimism indicates it is: a disposition to hope for the best, a tendency to look at the bright side, and a belief that good will predominate over evil.

This conjures up the picture of some poor schmuck sitting, eyes closed, and fingers crossed, praying everything will be all right. And business isn't Sunday school. So thinking good will triumph over evil is naïve at best. I don't know about you but I've seen a lot of bad people predominate over a lot of good people. In general, I do believe good does triumph over evil, but it's irrelevant to success or failure in business.

The only aspect of Webster's definition that makes the least bit sense in business is the tendency to look at the bright side. Even I can't argue with that. However, that doesn't mean I think such an attitude is all that beneficial.

I'm not interested in people who hope things will work out. I want people who know the issues, have thought through the possibilities, and are confident in their ability to succeed.

Let me share a couple of experiences where optimism actually hurt companies. Both examples have to do with bringing new technologies/products to market. They are complementary examples because one relates to over-estimating profitability and the other illustrates a situation where revenues were overstated. It's important to realize that optimism is not just related to sales or revenues. The dangers of being overly optimistic can create problems in many areas of business.

For the first example, let's return to the videoconferencing company. To refresh your memory our objective was to start a new division and grow an entirely new market segment for the company. The company had established itself by selling large, expensive conference room systems. Our charter was to take the same technology and port it to a PC platform. The theory was the world has many more desktops than conference rooms and ultimately that's where the lion's share of the videoconferencing market was going to migrate.

A sound premise. One I still believe will ultimately be realized.

What went wrong? Despite growing the revenue from zero to over $70 million in just three years we were losing money. Now you say, this was a new business and you would not necessarily expect profitability in less than five years. This was certainly the case in videoconferencing since the technology and the market had to mature. The problem was, management believed we could be profitable within two years, an extremely optimistic viewpoint.

I remember having a conversation with my boss, the division head, shortly after the initial business plan was approved. I told him it was basically impossible to achieve profitability within two years. There were far too many obstacles, not the least of which was the need to continue a heavy investment in research and development (R&D). There I go being negative. Where is that *can do* attitude? Terrible me, I let reality cloud my thinking once again.

Needless to say, two years came and went and we weren't anywhere near being profitable. There were a host of reasons. I mentioned the R&D issue. We were taking a very expensive technology and trying to make it relatively inexpensive. Our first product cost $6,000 and was expensive to build because our volumes were low. In order to achieve our market objectives we needed to get the price to below $1,500. That would cost a great deal of money.

We also needed to develop all new distribution channels and create a name for ourselves in the market. These were expensive and lengthy undertakings. There were numerous other reasons, but the reasons for not being profitable are not important.

What is important is our lack of profitability was predictable from the outset. Management's unbridled optimism left us operating in crisis mode after two years. Senior management wondered what had gone wrong.

Worse yet, we had a great deal of explaining to do to the investment community as to why our division was continuing to drag down the bottom line of the company. Oh yes, we told the investors we would be profitable. How's that for optimism. You can imagine the effort that was put in to spinning that story.

We did get a reprieve when an extra year was tacked on to our profitability goal, but it didn't matter. At that point, it was just delaying the inevitable because the same issues were still going to exist in a year. When the clock struck twelve on our one-year extension, the company panicked and virtually pulled the plug on the effort. Three years of very hard work by some very good people went completely up in smoke.

Could this have been avoided if a more realistic viewpoint were adopted initially? My boss said if he didn't promise profitability within two years the project would have never gotten off the ground. That was his rationale for making a commitment he knew was next to impossible to deliver. He thought it was better to make the commitment and hope for the best.

Well guess what? It wasn't better. The company would have been much better off never having tried. False expectations killed the project and inflicted a near-fatal wound to the company. From that point, the company began to spiral down. The failure of our division was not the sole reason or even the primary one, but it certainly didn't help.

The decision to move to the PC platform was absolutely the right decision at the time. Nothing that has transpired since has changed the fact it was the right thing to do. If the company had had a *realistic* understanding of what it would take and had been willing to do what was necessary to achieve the goal, we would have ultimately succeeded.

A similar situation occurred with one of my consulting assignments. The assignment was with the leading publishing company in the technology space. One of the company's divisions produced market research targeted at the PC and telecommunications industry. Historically, they had sold this research to big companies in the form of large and very expensive databases.

They began to pursue the idea of taking their data and putting it in a form conducive to delivery over the Web. The theory was to package the information in *bite-size* pieces, allowing companies of all sizes to affordably purchase it on an *ala carte* basis. This would allow the company to dramatically broaden its target market from a handful of very large companies to almost every company in the PC and telecommunications space.

Again, a very sound idea. No one in the industry possessed the type of data this company possessed. Over time, we could envision marketing and sales people throughout the industry becoming regular customers. Given sufficient time, the project had the potential of doubling the company's revenue. That was the crux of the problem. Time.

I came into the project shortly before the expected launch. I had known, for many years, both the president of the company as well as the other key player on the project, a well respected and high-profile industry analyst. I also specialized in bringing new products to market, so the assignment seemed perfect.

The people involved were very talented and it looked like a project that had *winner* written all over it. The catch phrase around the water cooler was, *millions while we sleep*. This was a reference to the expectations the division and corporate headquarters had for the project. We believed that as soon as we turned on the e-commerce engine and started taking orders, money would just be rolling in 24 hours a day.

Unfortunately, by the time I arrived, numerous missteps had already occurred. One of the biggest was the fact a good portion of the budget had been consumed reinventing Web technology. The project was being driven by development and was a case of an engineering team with a new toy. Rather than piece together stable and existing technologies, they decided it would be wonderful if they could integrate every new whiz-bang gadget they could get their hands on. Little time was spent on the research content, which was the actual product.

Forced to move the launch date back, we managed to piece together enough viable content to go to market. Still, valuable time had been lost and the forecast the group had promised to headquarters was in jeopardy. But never fear, remember, *millions while we sleep*. When we turn this puppy on money would just roll in.

We turned it on all right. But instead of millions while we sleep it turned into a penny for your thoughts. The revenue stream was more like a drip and it became painfully obvious we were not going to make the forecast. To compound the problem, we had blown through the budget and the project was deep in the red.

Should all this have been anticipated? The answer is an emphatic yes. First of all, if there was any chance of quickly generating revenue, a great deal more thought needed to go into the planning stage. Although a reasonable job was done building a registered user base prior to going pay-per-view, there was no significant marketing done. Nor was the base of users pre-qualified. Most of the qualified registered users were existing customers who had already purchased the data in its more comprehensive form.

But even if a better job were done in the preliminary stages, it was not reasonable to assume the site could generate the required monthly revenue in such a short ramp period. Building a paying customer base takes time. There are very few things that can be done to significantly reduce that cycle short of spending huge amounts of money on promotional campaigns. In this case, the budget wasn't there nor would the business model have supported such expenditures.

What happened? When it became obvious we wouldn't come close to the expected revenue goals it was time to abandon ship. As a consultant and outsider, it was interesting to observe how quickly the management team began distancing themselves from the product. Almost overnight, it had become a cancer no one, internally, wanted to be associated with. Mind you, these were the same people who had over-hyped and over-promised.

None of this was done maliciously. Management honestly believed it could accomplish the goals. This was simply a case of coming up with a very good idea and believing everyone would flock to it. It was a "build-it-and-they-will-come" philosophy. Unfortunately, that only works in the movies. No one asked the hard questions, no one prioritized the deliverables, no one lined up the necessary internal and external support, and no one had a sense of what was realistically possible given the relatively new delivery mechanism of the Web.

To compound the problem, the mother ship, whose primary revenue source was from advertising and trade shows, began to run into financial difficulties. It was slash and burn time and any project not pulling its weight was in deep trouble. The inevitable occurred and a promising idea was shelved.

Would it have been different if the corporation had not run into larger financial problems? Probably not. The damage was done when the expectations were set too high. In all likelihood, the disappointment would have been too great to overcome.

If these examples are not enough to convince you of the importance of being realistic versus being optimistic let me try another approach that may be easier to relate to. Let's say you're looking for financial advice to develop your stock portfolio. Would you seek out an investment advisor who believed everything was going to be great and didn't understand the risks involved with the recommended investments? Or would you want an advisor who did his or her homework, understood the fact that any investment is subject to risk, and explained the risks so you could make a fully informed decision?

Or what if you had a medical problem and had numerous options to choose from. Would you want a doctor who blindly believed good would triumph over evil? Or would you want one who could thoroughly explain the pros and cons of your various choices so you could understand the potential risks involved.

I can't speak for you but if I faced those situations, I would want someone who has thought about all the potential pitfalls. I don't want an optimist. I want a realist. Why should our approach to business be any different?

How can these kinds of situations be avoided? That's a difficult question because it is highly dependent on whether management is receptive to listening. In the case of the videoconferencing company, it could not have been avoided. This was an example of both politics and personal motivations clouding good business judgment.

My boss didn't believe he could persuade his colleagues in senior management and he wasn't willing to risk his *political capital* in an attempt. Despite continuing conversations, I was unable to gain any support for modifying our plan. Our only recourse was to proceed and do the best we could. Sometimes, that's all you can do.

The good news is, that's not always the case and the best way to increase your chances of convincing management is to do your homework. Remember: *confidence, preparation, and realism are the keys to success.*

In this case, *preparation* means analyzing the situation. Gather as much data as you can. Look at similar markets and products and examine historical forecasts if they exist. Make sure you thoroughly assess the dynamics of the product. For example, does the product fit your existing distribution channel? If not, this will impact how fast the product will ramp because it takes time to develop new channels. You need to evaluate all aspects of the business (development, sales, and the promotional requirements) to determine if they fit the product. You also need to ensure you have adequate resources to accomplish your objectives.

If you're faced with the challenge of bringing an entirely new product or technology to market, as was the case in both the videoconferencing and market research examples, there won't be any historical forecasts available. In this situation you may need to rely on third party market research. If you do, temper their forecasts. By this I mean try and *calibrate their accuracy.*

Calibrating accuracy can be accomplished by analyzing the track record of the research company. Look at how accurate they have been in the past. For example, you may find they have a tendency to miss their forecast on the high side by an average of 20 percent. Take this number and reduce their forecast by that amount before creating your forecast. If possible, try to get data from multiple sources. This will allow you to compare data and look for commonality. It will also allow you to use an averaging technique to develop a more realistic forecast upon which to base your business plan.

In general, my advice is to try to temper the natural enthusiasm that comes with any new project. If you're going to err, err on the side of being conservative. Why? When an initial business plan is formulated, revenues, profits or losses, and expense are all forecasted. Taking a conservative stance on the forecast will serve to hold expenses down. Then, if you miss the forecast the financial impact to the business is somewhat minimized. If you happen to beat the forecast, everyone will be ecstatic. You can always increase your expenditures once the revenue begins to flow.

Keep in mind, management will not welcome with open arms a downsized forecast. Before you present your findings make sure you have data to support your arguments. Try to anticipate the kinds of questions management will ask in the same way trial lawyers prepare witnesses. By doing so, you will present the image of being well *prepared* and *confident* in your findings. That will go a long way toward gathering support. Your hope is for management to listen. If they don't, then you will be faced with one of those hard career decisions.

CHAPTER SEVEN

Image is Everything Including Expensive

Before we tackle this chapter's subject, I'd like to discuss a change in direction. When I started this book I didn't intend to integrate sports to any significant degree. I knew I would invariably use a sprinkling of sports analogies because I use them in my day-to-day business life. But as the book progressed, I realized the parallels between the two worlds were even greater than originally thought.

One night, I decided it might not be a bad idea to combine the two. It was a basic marketing decision. I figured I could handle that. I've made enough of them in my life. Combining sports and business might distinguish the book from the hundreds of other business books being published. The downside was potentially alienating part of the target market.

Would I lose a significant part of the female demographic? Maybe, but it wasn't a given. Women are more interested in sports and vice versa. To broaden their appeal, teams and events allocate significant marketing dollars to attract the female audience. The ranks of sportscasters and commentators are no longer the purview of men. Women now participate in almost every broadcast, either from the studio or from the sidelines.

There was also the possibility the book would become more attractive to the male audience. I certainly could count on it being stronger with the cross-section of people interested in both business and sports.

That just left those women or men who aren't knowledgeable or have no interest in sports. Even with this market segment the decision could be beneficial. If I executed properly, the book could help them understand why there is a tendency to compare sports and business so often. It could be a win-win for all involved.

This is where the intangible of intuition plays a role in marketing. I was not about to formally research the market segmentation. I had neither the time nor the money. For this, I relied on gut instincts and decided placing a larger emphasis on sports would enhance the value of the book. Intuitively, I concluded the cross-section of sports enthusiasts in business was a fairly large target. I further concluded the potential loss of readers completely uninterested in sports would be relatively small. In my gut, the potential gain outweighed the downside and the decision was made.

Therefore take notice: this book has officially been repositioned. The main focus continues to be an examination of the political and cultural influences in business and the role of marketing, and combined with this will be a secondary focus on the parallels between sports and business.

A lesson can be learned from this decision. Writing this book is like bringing any product to market. It is a constantly evolving process. More often than not, the original concept is altered based upon changing conditions. Keep that in mind. A marketing strategy should never be cast in stone. To enhance the chances for success you need to continually test the pulse of the market, monitor competitors, observe the general economic and cultural environments, and be sufficiently flexible to react quickly and accurately.

Now, on with the subject at hand: image and branding as it relates to both sports and business.

As I was watching the National Basketball Association (NBA) finals I realized that I had been influenced by the initial image I had formed of Allen Iverson, a young and emerging Philadelphia 76ers star. Like many people, I made some quick judgments about his appearance and actions on and off the court. I had concluded that

Iverson was just another selfish punk, lacking discipline and only concerned with his own statistics.

It was difficult for me to come to any other conclusion. The cornrows and tattoos elicited images of street gangs and *gansta* rappers. Hell, Iverson even made a rap CD with reportedly controversial lyrics. Honestly, I don't know if the CD talked about killing authority figures or abusing women. Those seem to be recurring themes in a lot of rap music. It didn't matter, though, because just the fact he made a rap CD and looked like so many other unsavory rappers created a negative image in my mind. Fair or not I was influenced by his appearance.

The reason for all the talk about what a terrific player he is eluded me. He was being touted as a most valuable player (MVP) candidate and he was on pace to vie for the league's scoring title. Still, I'm thinking *what is all the hype about?* All this guy does is throw up shots regardless of where he is on the court. Anyone can lead the league in scoring if they take enough shots. Give me a break. Iverson was shooting 42 percent from the field. That's horrible even by today's standards. Of the top 50 scorers for that season only eight had a lower field-goal percentage. The league average was just over 44 percent. So the fact Iverson led the league in scoring had nothing to do with talent. At least that's what I thought.

Being a Knicks fan made it easier to dislike Iverson. OK, for those of you who don't follow basketball, the New York Knicks and Philadelphia 76ers are natural enemies. And given the fact that my Knicks performed dreadfully in the playoffs I wasn't in the mood to be generous in my opinion of rival players.

But something didn't jibe. As I watched the 76ers play I realized this kid and his teammates were the gutsiest bunch of competitors I had seen in a long time. They were well coached but the team didn't have much natural talent. They had gotten to the NBA finals on heart and sheer determination. The intangibles that tend to separate the good teams and players from the great teams and players. That's something you don't see very often these days. Today, with the big salaries and the *prima dona* attitudes few professional athletes exhibit the kind of effort the 76ers put forth. It was a throw back to days gone by.

More importantly, the team's determination all flowed from Iverson. During the entire game he never let up, throwing his body into a forest of men virtually twice his size. You got the impression he would sacrifice anything to win and that's what sports is all about. Even his poor shooting could be accounted for by the fact his team was not very good and he was forced to take so many shots in order to have a chance to win. Granted, Iverson is not a great shooter but he isn't as bad as his statistics would lead one to believe.

Why am I telling you this? The point is, despite the mountain of press Iverson had gotten through the course of the year, he had an image problem with me (and many other non-76er fans). It was not until I could focus on his ability and heart that that image began to turn. Iverson makes millions of dollars and certainly has some high-powered publicists working for him, but it took the concentrated exposure of the NBA finals for him to start overcoming his less-than-desirable image. That is the point.

Image building and company branding are ticklish business. I've seen too many companies make the same mistake. As mentioned before, it seems when companies approach $500 million in revenues they get an urge to *brand* themselves. They can't seem to help but hire a high profile ad agency to create an advertising campaign designed to put them on the map.

Unfortunately, branding campaigns are very expensive propositions. We touched upon it briefly in the first chapter. To execute an effective branding campaign, you need a large financial war chest and you need the patience to see it through. There are no shortcuts to branding. It takes time. A lot of time.

It doesn't matter how big you are. A company cannot create a ubiquitous image without money and time.

At $500 million in revenues it's almost impossible to do. Companies that size rarely have the resources to pull it off. But alas, invariably the egos of the management team flare up and they decide they want to increase the company's profile. My advice to any company with less than a billion dollars in revenue: *don't even think about executing a branding campaign.* The best way to brand the company at that stage is to sell more product.

To illustrate the point, I want to share with you one of the most successful branding campaigns ever conducted. It serves as an excellent example of just what kind of resources and company stature it takes to create a corporate image recognized by the population as a whole.

The campaign I'm referring to is the *Intel Inside®* campaign. For the 6 percent of the population unfamiliar with Intel, they are, among other things, the leading microprocessor company in the world. Most PCs are *powered* by Intel's Pentium® processor.

When Intel first launched the campaign, I thought they were crazy. Why would anyone care about the processor in the PC as long as all their software worked? Those of us in the industry knew there was little difference among the available processors, and software compatibility wasn't really an issue. True, Intel was by far the dominant player, but other companies had developed comparable technology and the competitive products were significantly less expensive.

The mistake I made was being a bit too informed. At the time, the majority of customers had concerns. To most businesses, the security inherent in choosing Intel was well worth the added cost. Over time this has changed. Businesses and the general consumer population are now more knowledgeable, and price sensitive. As a consequence, AMD (Advanced Micro Devices) was able to establish itself as a viable competitor of Intel by offering lower cost solutions.

The key point is, the fact that the consumer *should* not have cared did not mean they *would* not care. It's important, when looking at issues like this, to step back and not bias your opinion with inside knowledge. Never impose the enhanced level of knowledge you may possess on the general buying public. That's a lesson it took me years to learn.

By and large, the public can be convinced of all kinds of things that in reality are nothing more than hype. That's part of marketing's role. As long as you don't lie in the process, it's all fair game.

Joining the industry in our skepticism regarding Intel's campaign was the media. They raised doubts about whether a component-based technology company like Intel could successfully execute this kind of marketing campaign. Intel didn't sell anything directly to consumers. And branding like this is usually reserved for the likes of big consumer companies such as Ford, McDonalds and Wal-Mart. We were both wrong.

Intel launched the campaign in 1991. They were already almost a $5 billion company with net income of more than $800 million. Clearly they had reached the threshold of launching a successful branding campaign. On top of that, they dominated their market and had every major PC manufacturer on the planet in their camp. They were dealing from an enviable position of strength. They definitely had the ante, as it were, to mount such an ambitious campaign.

But even with all of these plusses, Intel had to have some nagging doubts about what it was undertaking. Though they were a large and dominant company, known by everyone in the industry and many in the business community, the average consumer had no idea who they were. This would be the first time any technology component manufacturer had attempted to brand itself with consumers. They were breaking new ground and that always leads to uncertainty.

Being a component manufacturer increased Intel's challenge. However, unlike most component manufacturers, Intel had an advantage. At the time, when someone went to buy a computer, the first criteria was the brand of the manufacturer, whether it was IBM, Compaq, or Dell. The vast majority of consumers didn't buy a PC because of who made the disk drive, display or microprocessor. There was one exception.

Although they didn't necessarily know or care who made the processor, they did care about the type of processor. The processor is the *engine* of the PC. As such, a consumer would choose a PC based on processor type because it signified the PC's power. It was common for people to refer to PCs as a Compaq 386 or an IBM 486, or sometimes just as a 386 or 486. But the name Intel wasn't usually associated with it. The reputation of the manufacturer whose name was on the outside of the PC was the critical decision factor. Intel wanted to change this.

Cars serve as a good analogy. When most people buy a car they don't worry about who made the muffler, water pump, or fuel injector. Just as with Intel's processor, they may care about some of the engine's *characteristics* like horsepower or the number of cylinders, but again, their interest tends to end there.

There are some car components like the sound system and tires consumers also show interest in but only because of external issues. These components get attention because they are visible or audible. The value of the stereo is directly related to the quality of the sound and tires influence both safety and performance.

This makes brand a factor, but a secondary one. The reason for this is because the brand of the individual components tends to be consistent with the manufacturer's brand. For example, you would expect high performance tires and sound systems in a BMW.

Thus, by and large, people buy cars based on the manufacturer brand.

This concept might have influenced Intel and its partners. If Intel could successfully brand itself as the high quality, high performance processor, Intel's PC partners would benefit by being able to position the PCs they manufactured as high quality and high performance. This would allow them to command a higher price and potentially higher margins. A good thing for everyone involved.

The idea to launch the Intel campaign was initiated in 1989 when a small group was formed to create a program to market the 386SX chip to information technology (IT) managers in the business community. According to Intel, the effort was successful, but legal problems arose as the courts ruled Intel could not trademark the generic names 386 and 486.

This forced Intel to alter its strategy from branding the product to branding the company. This was a critical turning point. Ironically, what the company probably perceived as a setback turned into one of the biggest breaks imaginable and another example of a situation where you might rather be lucky than good. It's also another example of a company that made its own luck. If Intel never attempted to brand itself none of this would have mattered. Preparation meeting opportunity equals success.

After analyzing successful campaigns, and working in conjunction with their advertising agency, the tag line *Intel Inside* was born. The strategy was to associate Intel with technology leadership, reliability, and safety. This is vintage Intel. What that really meant is FUD: fear uncertainty and doubt. Place the seed in the consumer's mind that any other choice is risky. Perhaps one of those other processors wouldn't run your favorite application correctly. That won't happen with Intel.

Granted, if you bought an Intel-based PC you didn't have to

worry about compatibility problems, but that was 99.9 percent true for other manufacturers as well. There were stories about software not running properly on other processors. For the vast majority of consumers there wasn't anything to worry about. Today, software compatibility is a non-issue. Intel differentiates itself based on speed, features, and the strength of the brand.

The strategy was brilliant and the timing was perfect. Intel's competitors were relatively weak and the average consumer was not sophisticated enough to challenge Intel's position. Intel could easily outspend the competition, drowning them in a sea of marketing. All without possessing any appreciable product differentiation. From a marketing standpoint, you have to love it. It's what marketing people live for; making something out of nothing.

The campaign focused around a co-op program targeted at PC manufacturers. Co-op programs are widely used in retail distribution. They basically provide marketing dollars to partners who, in turn, are required to perform certain actions. In the case of the *Intel Inside* campaign, any PC manufacturer willing to put the *Intel Inside* logo on the outside of the PC would get 5 percent of the cost of the processor put in a fund the PC manufacturer could use for print advertising. That is as long as that advertising also included the Intel logo. Basically, it was a legal bribe. You put my name on your PC and I give you money to be used for advertising that will benefit both of us.

That is one of the catches to co-op programs. You don't actually get hard cash. What you get is the ability to accrue funds to be spent under the program's guidelines. Typically, there is also a time period in which the funds need to be spent or lost. But this is a minor constraint. The PC manufacturers were able to supplement their own advertising dollars with Intel's money by doing little more than putting a sticker on the outside of the PC. Everyone benefited, and as a result, by the end of 1991, three hundred PC companies had signed up to support the program.

This was probably the most critical factor in the success of the campaign. Intel had control of almost the entire base of PC manufacturers. That gave them a tremendous amount of leverage. None of their competitors could hope to come close to countering the power Intel had with the vendors. And the program was designed in such a way it almost guaranteed participation. Every planet and star was aligning.

Intel then went for the knockout punch. For that, they deserve a great deal of credit. As a company, they have an admirable *killer instinct.* I don't always agree with their ethics or their tactics, but I do appreciate a company who knows how to finish the job. All too often companies ease up, thinking they have won before they have actually put their opponents away. And just as often they end up getting blindsided by those very same competitors.

This has strong parallels with sports. The killer instinct is what separates the truly great from the very good. This is particularly true in boxing but applies to all sports. In boxing, many talented fighters just don't know how to finish off an opponent. They allow them to linger, which is definitely not a good thing when someone is trying to knock you silly.

In team sports it's not unusual for a team to get a big lead, but only a few know how to hold a lead and put their adversary away. Those teams tend to be the ones who win championships. The same holds true in the business world. It's one thing to get your opponent down, after that you have to finish them off. Intel and Microsoft are two companies who do that better than most.

What was Intel's knockout punch? In addition to the co-op program, they started a worldwide print advertising campaign targeted directly at the consumer. This was an effort to reinforce the story behind the logo. Then, in 1992, they ran their first TV ad. In 1995, the now famous five-tone jingle was born, and now the popular *Blue Man Group* has been used to tout the Pentium 4 processor.

What were the results? In late 1991, Intel estimated only 24 percent of European PC buyers were familiar with the *Intel Inside* logo. One year later, that number grew to 80 percent and reached 94 percent by 1995. By the late 1990s the program was widely hailed as a resounding success. The Intel brand became known worldwide and its name is now synonymous with the PC industry.

What were the costs? To achieve this success Intel and the computer manufacturers invested over $7 billion in advertising. As of this writing, approximately 2,700 PC manufacturers are licensed to use the Intel logo. And Intel's investment continues. The company expected to spend $1.5 billion in 2001 to perpetuate the campaign.

Could such a campaign work as well if launched today? Not likely. Consumers are more knowledgeable and Intel's competitors are a bit stronger. But that's all the more reason for Intel to continue to invest. Now, more than ever, it's important for them to maintain the advantage they've created and not assume it will just continue. Intel is applying Andy Grove's philosophy: *only the paranoid survive*. More on this later.

What did it take for an established and cash rich company like Intel to become a household name? It took time. It was six years from the original idea, in 1989, until it achieved the 94 percent recognition figure in Europe in 1995. It took money. Seven billion and counting – not to mention the fact Intel possessed a dominant market position and executed its campaign flawlessly. That's what it took.

The point is, a company with revenues equal to half of Intel's net profits should not be contemplating a branding effort. If you ever find yourself in a company around $500 million in size and management gets antsy to brand themselves, maybe sharing this story might help persuade them to wait and focus on making a name for themselves by selling more product.

As an employee, do some research and use examples like this to convey the seriousness of the investment in both time and money required to be successful. Look at comparable companies as well as competitors to see if any of them have successfully executed a branding campaign. Possibly, if management is presented with profiles of companies who have successfully branded themselves versus those who didn't, they will be in a more informed position to make the right decision.

Challenge the ad agency, and whoever else may be involved in creating the campaign, to thoroughly analyze the situation. Any campaign should include definitive and measurable goals. Ensure the campaign strategy is valid by *encouraging* those responsible to outline why they believe it can be successful given the available resources. Are you reaching enough people? Will you be able to achieve the necessary frequency with the target audience? How likely is the target audience to see and read the ads?

Although it's unlikely you'll get anything useful, ask for data on similar companies and campaigns. And remember, any ad agency or outside vendor who agrees to take on the assignment will obviously be in favor of the campaign. It represents a revenue opportunity for them. Understand their biases and factor them in.

It also may help to discuss with management the opportunity costs involved in allocating resources toward branding versus programs that are more apt to impact immediate sales. Offer alternative strategies that may enhance the company's market position and equip them for a branding effort down the road. You may not be able to change management's mind but that doesn't mean you shouldn't try. Do your homework, make others do their homework, present the facts, and let the chips fall where they may.

CHAPTER EIGHT

The Internet: Fact Versus Fiction

A conversation with a recent college graduate caused me to reflect upon the roller coaster ride known as the Internet. As with most recent graduates, the young woman was enthusiastic about the opportunities that lay ahead. Her degree was in Internet Marketing, a highly sought after skill with an abundance of career choices. Or so she and most everyone else thought.

What struck me were her perceptions of the Internet and what she had obviously been taught during her college tenure. Her professors elevated the Internet to mythical proportions. It was obvious they too had bought into all the hype foisted on the public.

This wasn't a shock. Hell, most of the people in academia have little or no practical experience. Many have been academics all their lives. If they were ever in the commercial sector it was likely so many years ago they have lost touch. Worse yet, many have held nothing but staff positions high above the fray. You know the ones: director of strategic planning, manager of corporate development. The only time these people ever rolled up their sleeves was to wash their hands of the companies they helped screw up. In all my years I still haven't figured out what they contribute. They're all theory, and constantly try to apply textbook concepts to the real world.

Fortunately, there are exceptions, teachers with experience in the trenches, who truly understand the business world. More often than not they tend to teach at night because they have day jobs that provide a true teaching foundation. I consider myself lucky to have earned my degrees at night. I actually learned some useful things from people who lived what they taught.

But sadly, if you get your degree the usual way, during the day, most of what you learn in business school is useless. Oh it's good for understanding the fundamentals of the various disciplines such as marketing, finance, statistics, business law, and the like. But it falls woefully short of accurately portraying the realities of business. So the fact they were getting it wrong in the classroom when it came to marketing on the Internet was not a revelation.

Even the idea of majoring in Internet Marketing is a bit absurd to me. Do you think marketing on the Internet is that different from marketing in general? The vast majority of marketing principles apply in all situations, including the Internet. The differences are no greater than those that exist between developing print versus TV advertising.

Basically, the Internet is nothing more than another means to interact and communicate with your customers and partners. The medium is different, requiring changes in technique. The jargon is certainly different as are the measurements of success. That, by and large, is the extent of it. The differences in the Internet may be worthy of a course, but not an entire college career.

The frenzy surrounding the Internet was completely out of control. It was surreal in nature, as if we had entered another dimension. Companies were changing their names to have dot-something in it, believing that alone would enhance the value of their stock. Start-ups blew a million bucks in a single day to advertise during the Super Bowl.

Sure, all new technologies are over hyped. It comes with the territory. The next one in line is the 3G wireless technology. Don't hold your breath waiting for that to happen. The Internet was different though. This one brought hype to new levels.

The Internet's hype far exceeded any previous technology.

Coming on the heels of the Y2K extravaganza, that was no easy feat. Y2K was classic. The world was going to come to an end because a bunch of applications were going to get confused as to what year it was. I can't tell you how many intelligent people expressed their concerns to my better half and me about the potential catastrophic impact. I mean black outs, planes falling out of the sky, stuff like that.

These crazy ideas didn't usually come from people in the industry. No, the industry was generally divided into two camps: people who knew it wasn't a major issue and those who saw an opportunity to make money by trying to convince people it was.

Before you get started, yes there were legitimate problems with a small percentage of applications. The problem was primarily with older programs, many written in COBOL. And there's no denying a good deal of the affected software was deployed in mission-critical applications such as banking and government.

But we weren't talking about major bugs or intrinsically flawed software code. We were talking about fixing a problem with the freaking date. The biggest challenge was the sheer number of lines of code that needed to be reviewed. Fixing it was tedious work, but it didn't require an army of geniuses. There was never a real threat. It just made for good copy and it made a handful of people some money. All in all, this was a relatively harmless and short-term glitch for society.

Not so with the Internet. The hype over the Internet has had a broader and longer-term impact. It has done real harm not just to individuals, but to the economy as a whole. The overblown belief that the Internet offered the ability to create an entirely new economy impacted investment decisions and stock prices. And it influenced sales and revenue forecasts of companies supplying technology for the Internet like telecommunication companies. When this artificial bubble burst, it had a huge ripple effect. Moving forward, it is imperative that we under-stand the Internet for what it is, and recognize its true benefits.

My purpose here is to try and communicate those benefits and explore, in general terms, how businesses can leverage them. The value of understanding the Internet and how to leverage it as a business tool is not restricted to the high tech industry. Every company in every industry, whether they are large or small, can effectively use the Internet if they understand how. The value is also not restricted only to those in marketing. We can all benefit, both professionally and personally, from the Internet and World Wide Web.

Let's put the Internet and World Wide Web in perspective. Fundamentally the Internet is two things: it is another form of distribution and it is a new and more efficient way of disseminating and exchanging information. OK, maybe that's three things. In any event, this isn't trivial, but it's not completely earth shattering either. The Internet will certainly enhance productivity. It will also allow some companies to compete that would not otherwise have a viable means to do so. Important? Yes. A paradigm shift? Yes. A completely new way of doing business? No.

The collective Internet can be boiled down to five basic uses or applications:

1. The world's largest electronic catalogue;
2. The world's biggest billboard;
3. The world's most impressive library;
4. A mechanism to communicate and transact with customers, distribution partners, vendors, and suppliers; and
5. (Someday) the world's greatest source of entertainment

Now that sounds impressive doesn't it? Let's look as each of these applications individually and understand their potential impact.

The Internet or more correctly the World Wide Web is *the*

world's largest electronic catalogue. Hard to argue with that. E-commerce and many of the dot-coms revolved around selling products via the Internet. In essence, they were and are online catalogues; fundamentally no different than the catalogues you receive in the mail. The Internet is a more efficient means of providing at home catalogue shopping.

From the consumer's standpoint we now have access to a virtually unlimited number of catalogues with an enhanced level of information. Not only do they get high quality photographs, but in many cases three-dimensional views or video to help embellish the product description. The consumer can also search for specific items much easier, no longer having to flip through an index to find items scattered throughout a paper catalogue.

For vendors, the cost of creating and distributing product information is greatly reduced. And as important, electronic catalogues can easily be kept current, whereas updating printed catalogues is difficult and expensive. Vendors also benefit from the ability to track customer preferences and more easily capture detailed customer demographics. This allows them to develop a better understanding of their customers and more effectively target marketing campaigns. For example, customers can be easily notified when products or services of particular interest become available or are discounted.

All in all this is a win-win. But is it life altering? Is it cause to say this represents a whole new economy? Does it warrant the kind of hype and attention the Internet has received? Evidently to some. I may be jaded by having spent so many years in high tech but I view this more as evolutionary than revolutionary. It is a natural progression based upon technological advancements. It is more akin to the advancement made from the pony express to the mail service. More information available to more people, more cost effectively.

What about the Internet and Web as *the world's biggest billboard?* Most of the same benefits apply here. If used properly the Internet is the most efficient way to communicate all kinds of information about a company and its products. No longer do companies need an army of telesales reps answering questions and sending out literature. All of this can be accomplished via the Internet. Product information, customer service information, investor relations, and even hiring information can all be accessed via the Web.

From the consumer's standpoint they now have access to information for companies throughout the world. They don't have to make phone calls or wait for information to be sent through the mail. They can download files and even hear what senior management is saying. They can listen to conference and earning calls and correspond via e-mail. All of which saves people time and money.

For the vendor this amounts to a huge cost savings. It is not so much that they are providing *new* information, though in some cases they are. For the most part they can provide *better* information, more of it, and in a more timely fashion. For example, they can now disseminate video clips from management, product demos, and online training. In general, the Internet allows information to be distributed more efficiently.

Companies save on staffing in many departments including marketing, sales, finance, and perhaps human resources. They save on the cost of mailing literature and other company information. They may even eliminate expensive marketing tactics such as trade shows since the need to attend these types of industry events diminishes with the availability of online information.

Companies can also better track customers and their behavior. They can run trial marketing and promotional campaigns over the

Internet prior to any full launch. This allows them to fine tune their marketing efforts and maximize resources.

It all adds up to better marketing, better communications, and better customer service, while simultaneously reducing the associated costs. A very cool thing if you run a business. And the beauty of it is you can accomplish these things regardless of whether you are big or small. Big companies could always afford to service their customers, but historically, smaller organizations have had to forego many marketing services. To a degree, the Internet levels the playing field.

Then there's *the Internet as a library*. This is the capability I have found most attractive. As a consultant, collecting information on a company or market is a critical component to doing the job. In the past, information would have to be requested by calling individual companies. Acquiring the necessary research may have meant a trip to the library. The old way was tedious and time consuming. With the Web it's a simple matter of typing in a URL or doing a search. Invariably, the right information can be found. I can do in hours what it might have taken days to do before.

And the library-like nature of the Internet does not just apply to business. Everything from planning a vacation to studying the mating habits of a fruit fly can be accessed from the Internet. (I'm guessing about the fruit fly thing. OK wait. So nobody can accuse me of not doing my homework it took all of two minutes to find a site detailing the habits of fruit flies and every other fly you can imagine. Did you know fruit flies are also known as vinegar flies? You learn something every day.)

Someday, there will be no brick-and-mortar libraries. You'll find everything you could ever hope for on the Internet and books will be printed on demand. Not any time soon but within the next hundred years or so. A hundred years! Am I crazy? We can do all that now. True, but the fact we can do it today is inconsequential. Society just does not move that fast. Old ways of doing things don't die easily, and replacing all the libraries in the world with PCs and the Internet assumes everyone has a PC and can access the Internet, not just in the United States but the world. We're looking at somewhere around hundred years if not more.

These three applications fall into the category of *business-to-consumer* communications or B2C. However, in an industry that never lacks for acronyms we also need to discuss the *business-to-business* communications or B2B applications.

Just as the Internet provides a comprehensive means for companies to communicate and transact business directly with their customers, it offers this capability for business-to-business communications. There are a myriad of potential transactions and communications that occur between businesses, most of which can be done more efficiently over the Internet.

For example, a business can order raw materials online. Better yet, a supplier with the proper security can access a company's internal inventory management system to see if there are any material needs. Sales orders from distribution partners can be processed and scheduled online versus by paper or by phone. The possibilities are endless and a plethora of companies are offering technology to facilitate this B2B environment – everything from Customer Relationship Management (CRM), to Sales Force Automation (SFA), to Enterprise Resource Planning (ERP). I told you there is no lack of acronyms.

It should be noted the Internet was not the first implementation of such electronic communications. Before the Internet and World Wide Web many companies began to implement electronic data interchange or EDI. EDI was the first form of businesses conducting transactions electronically among themselves. The concept of EDI along with the applications mentioned above are being extended to the Web and will ultimately make businesses more efficient and help minimize errors by reducing or eliminating paper and phone transactions.

Certainly a very good thing but hardly any of this is new. It can be likened to the impact the fax machine had on businesses. Before the fax, sales orders, contracts, and the like were mailed. The fax eliminated the time it took to mail documents making businesses more efficient. That's what the Internet does.

Last but not least, the Internet as a *vehicle for entertainment.* A bunch of companies are chasing this pot of gold. Some day it will happen. The Internet has the potential to deliver any form of entertainment on an on-demand basis.

However, the Internet is at the mercy of our communications infrastructure. It is this dependency that will continue to inhibit the ability of the Internet to realize its full potential. This is despite the fact there is no lack of content. Nor is cost an issue with powerful PCs selling for under $1,000 and Internet access costing around $25 per month.

Ah, but alas, we can't gloss over the infrastructure problem. Of all the problems to have, it's got to be the worst one. It is the Internet's Achilles heel. Why? Because it will cost a huge amount of money to fix. More money than any one company can afford to spend. Just ask the telecommunications and cable companies. They have already invested billions of dollars in upgrading their networks with little to show for it.

Even after all this investment, only a small percentage of the population has access to broadband technologies such as DSL. And without broadband, and I mean broadband that works, there is no way for the Internet to be an effective, affordable delivery mechanism for entertainment. The quality is not high enough and it takes too long to download files. The average person won't tolerate it.

I suspect it will take another 10 years or more for the infrastructure to improve sufficiently to deliver quality entertainment to the masses. There are many reasons for this but the biggest is money. It involves replacing existing copper wires with fiber or more likely wireless technologies.

We could go into all the various approaches of using existing copper and all the little tricks vendors have come up with to try and circumvent the problem. They all amount to nothing more than stopgap measures. Short of laying new cable to every home or developing a cost-effective high bandwidth wireless network, everything companies are doing today is intended to try to artificially accelerate a market while minimizing cost. It works for a segment of the population but not for the whole. So yes, some day the Internet will provide unprecedented levels of entertainment. Just don't expect it to happen in the next few years.

Even after the infrastructure problem is solved what will the Internet be capable of doing? The answer is, not much more than what your TV can do today. Let's put it in context. When TV usurped radio as the next big form of entertainment and information how earth shattering was it? Well, for starters it certainly was an improvement over its predecessor. TV added the visual element. A major leap forward.

Does the Internet add a totally new element? No. It can't even deliver the same level as TV. It will some day. Once it does, what will have happened? Your TV becomes a PC and vice versa. You won't get an entirely new *dimension* of information, you'll simply get more of it and any way you want it. You'll be able to schedule your entertainment easier, pause it, store it, and even get some incremental information like DVDs now provide.

The Internet will become the world's biggest and most

powerful remote control. Nice, yes. Life altering, not mine. It certainly will affect the media companies. That's why they are all scrambling to control the Internet and its associated content. This latter issue is more than a bit scary.

To sum it up, the Internet is a tremendous source of information. It provides better information, faster, and more economically than virtually any other source. It is a powerful marketing and communication tool. It will streamline many business processes. It will provide many companies with access to new markets and allow many more companies to compete. It provides consumers with greater choices and efficiencies. And someday, it will be the Mecca of the entertainment world.

This all sounds incredible, and in many ways it is. But I still contend it is evolutionary and not revolutionary. It represents more an automation of existing processes rather than an entirely new process. The Internet is a better mousetrap that adds up to a higher degree of efficiency, but not necessarily a whole new way of doing business, and certainly not a new economy.

The Internet cannot even be compared to perhaps the greatest technical innovation to date, the personal computer. The PC impacted businesses and consumers to a much greater degree than the Internet has or will. Heck, if it were not for the personal computer the Internet would be nothing more than what it started out to be, a network of networks for technical geeks.

The Internet does not fundamentally change basic business practices nor has it demonstrated an ability to create a vast array of new markets like the PC did. Funny, I don't remember anyone proclaiming a new economy had arrived when the first PC showed up. Perhaps those of us involved in the early days of the PC just did not understand the fundamentals of marketing and economics. Or then again, maybe we did.

CHAPTER NINE

David and Goliath Parts I & II

Before your career is over, odds are you'll find yourself working for a small to mid-size company. This may be for no other reason than most jobs are with smaller companies. The decision to work for a smaller rather than a bigger company is personal one. Everyone has to determine the environment best suited for them and the environment that will best serve their career goals. To make the right choice you need to understand the tradeoffs.

Working for a large company, particularly one that is widely recognized offers prestige and can make a resume more attractive. Large organizations have cachet. Frequently, they can better position a person to achieve senior management roles. This is similar to the benefit from attending an Ivy League university.

But, like everything in life, there are tradeoffs. Moving up the ladder in a large company takes longer. You also have to be prepared to take assignments that may be less than attractive to prove you are committed to the company. Patience is key. It will take longer to get things done on a day-to-day basis and it may take longer to build your career. The upside is you're likely to have more options if you have big company experience.

Smaller organizations tend to be more dynamic and freewheeling. Decisions and actions happen quicker and there is more opportunity to make an immediate impact. Getting a title and/or management responsibilities can happen faster with a small company. The chance to make a lot of money on stock options is also greater.

Companies of different sizes generally have different corporate cultures. Large companies are more regimented with clearly defined rules and processes, whereas smaller companies often operate more spontaneously. Many make it up as they go. Be aware of the cultural differences and decide which is best for you.

Despite having opportunities, I've limited my working relationship with large companies to consulting. My preference is smaller organizations because they better suit my personality and style. I wouldn't fit with the corporate culture of most large organizations; they just have too much bureaucracy, process, and politics for me. And quickly making a significant impact is next to impossible. For me, smaller organizations are simply more fun. Particularly when you get a chance to compete against the big boys.

That's the topic for this chapter, competing effectively against large organizations. Twice I've mixed it up with industry heavyweights. Those experiences were the most exciting of my career. It's a little like Rocky, you get your title shot and – win, lose, or draw – it's a rush.

PART I

The first battle took place in the mid-'80s while working with a leading PC enhancement company. The industry was in its early stage and was driven by hardware companies. Software applications were limited by the hardware and were relatively unsophisticated. Networking and communications technologies were just beginning to emerge. The World Wide Web wasn't even a gleam in anyone's eye. Then, hardware was the place to be just as the Internet is the place to be today.

My company was the market leader for PC enhancement products. They developed products such as memory boards, graphic controllers and networking cards. A mundane, commodity market today, but a high profile and influential market 15 years ago.

The company generated almost 90 percent of its revenues

from a line of memory-related products. Memory products were big business in those years for two reasons. First, memory was relatively expensive so the standard PC came with a minimal amount (64KB). Second, just as today, software applications were increasing in complexity and continually demanding more resources.

I joined the company to run marketing for the memory business unit. It was quite a responsibility since it was the company's bread and butter. The profits from this business funded the company's growth. A misstep could have major downside implications.

Due to limitations in DOS (disk operating system), applications could only address 640KB of RAM (random access memory). This was a mounting problem as applications increased in sophistication. Additional memory was needed to allow the software to grow in features and functions.

The technology industry has always been clever in devising ways to circumvent these kinds of problems. In this spirit of ingenuity, Intel, Microsoft, and Lotus collaborated on a new memory specification to make it possible to address 1MB of memory. Despite being a temporary solution, it would do until a permanent one could be found. It was called the Expanded Memory Specification (EMS) and was the hottest technology in the industry for over a year.

Intel was driving the specification. Their goal was to enter the PC add-on market with a line of memory products based on the new specification. This would put them head to head with my company and attack the heart of our business. Intel, of course, understood this. As a consequence, they decided to freeze us out of participating in the specification's development.

To make matters worse, they solicited and received the support of the two most powerful software companies of the time, Microsoft and Lotus. For those who don't know Lotus Development Corporation, they developed the Lotus 1-2-3 spreadsheet and dominated the spreadsheet market for many years until Microsoft overshadowed them. (They have since been acquired by IBM.)

This was a smart and aggressive move on Intel's part. The new hardware specification was useless without software support. They used their industry position to line up the two key players and virtually assure the specification would become an industry standard. If that happened, we were in danger of losing our leadership position, not to mention a huge piece of our revenue stream.

The founders of my company were livid. To a degree, they had a right to be. Many companies were permitted to comment on the specification prior to its release, but we were not one of them. We didn't receive the preliminary spec until it was released to the general vendor community. This was a slap in the face to the market leader.

As insulting as it was, Intel did the right thing. This wasn't a social club, it was business. If you intend to enter a new market why would you give any edge to the current market leader? At least we knew it was coming, we just didn't have much time to prepare.

What the hell were we going to do? Intel, one of the largest and most respected hardware companies in the industry was about to go after our core business and they had the support of the two biggest software companies in the world. Their specification was certain to be embraced. All we could do was hope to get a piece of the new business. Or maybe, we could kick them in the shins! Actually, I prefer to aim a little higher.

The technology industry was even more freewheeling than it is now. Nothing was guaranteed and we were not without resources. True, Intel was much bigger and more respected, but we had a fairly prominent name. More importantly, we had solid distribution channels and relationships. Also, Intel's size and influence did not totally compensate for the fact they were the new kid on the block when it came to selling memory.

Even so, they were a formidable challenge. We couldn't outspend them and our relationships couldn't match theirs. Plus, they had the support of the key software vendors and their name was on the specification. That was more than just a public relations problem. The specification would be known as the Lotus Intel Microsoft Expanded Memory Specification or LIM EMS. Quite a mouthful, but you see the problem. It made Intel look like the industry leader.

Despite this, we weren't going to roll over. *The first lesson in competing with a larger company is to be aggressive.* Being timid gets you nothing but walked on. By being aggressive you stand a fighting chance. The worst that can happen is you get crushed, but that would happen anyway. I'd rather go down with guns blazing. If nothing else, you can make them bleed before they get you. Luckily, our founders were an aggressive bunch. Better yet, they were plain pissed about the entire matter. It was personal with them allowing us to be unconstrained in our response.

Although we had been excluded initially, we had clever engineers and enough time to review the specification. We were able to assess our options before the official unveiling. The good news was the spec wasn't perfect, leaving room for improvements. And that's what we did. We improved it and quickly announced our own version. We called ours the EEMS or Double EMS. This stood for the Enhanced Expanded Memory Specification. Not bad, a little one-upsmanship. We had created a superset. Being a superset we had the ability to do everything their spec could do and more.

We still had one minor problem. Our spec may have been

better on paper but we couldn't prove it. We hadn't had time to identify a software developer who could or would support our enhancements. This left us at a distinct disadvantage.

Intel immediately went into FUD mode. FUD: fear, uncertainty, and doubt. Intel commonly employed the tactic. It involves trying to convince potential buyers it is risky to choose a competitive solution. They proceeded to tell anyone who would listen that our specification might not be fully compatible.

Now wait just a minute. *Thems* fighting words, not to mention a big problem if people believed Intel. The irony was Intel didn't believe it, but that never stopped them. FUD was their standard tactic. They knew there was nothing incompatible in our spec. Regardless, they were attempting to place doubt in the minds of prospective customers.

This is not behavior I condone. Business may be a war-like endeavor but even war has rules. You don't go around telling lies about your competitors to gain the upper hand. That's just wrong.

Wrong or right we had to deal with it. We had a two-pronged strategy. First, we would demonstrate we were not just compatible but better. Second, we would wage a war of words in the trade press.

Proving compatibility and superiority would take time. The software vendors who announced support for the new memory standard had not updated their software yet. This worked in Intel's favor. They could and would continue to claim ours did not work. There was simply no way of disproving their statement short of doing a thorough technical analysis of both specs. Dissecting the bits and bytes was impractical for the average user.

Fortunately there was one important avenue available. We could tell our story to the press. They were technically savvy and interested enough to listen. As a bonus, the press loves this kind of fight between companies. It makes for good copy.

With the compatibility issue left to the press we turned our attention to proving we had improved the specification. For that, we needed an application. Not just any application, we needed a sophisticated piece of software. Intel had already wrapped up support for the top two.

Microsoft had supported the EMS to help establish Microsoft® Windows®. Microsoft was in the early stages of establishing Windows, and they desperately needed more memory to facilitate one of its key features, the ability to run more than one task at the same time. At that point, PCs could only run a single application at a time. Windows would take PC computing to the next level.

The Lotus 1-2-3 spreadsheet was the leading software application in the market. It was so successful many credit it for helping make the PC the dominant computing platform. Outside of Lotus and Microsoft there weren't any other prominent software companies in a position to help. There was however, a little company called Quarterdeck.

Quarterdeck was a squirrelly, technically-driven company who developed a bubble-gum and bailing-wire version of an operating environment called DESQview. It also allowed multiple tasks to run simultaneously. The difference between DESQview and Windows was Windows was graphics-based and DESQview was character-based. It wasn't as sexy as Windows but it had one distinct advantage. It actually worked and Windows still had all sorts of problems. Windows was pushing the envelope of the hardware platform. It taxed the hardware and ran much slower than DESQview.

Quarterdeck was swimming against the tide. It was only a matter of time before Microsoft overwhelmed them. They simply didn't have the resources to compete. That is until we showed up with our enhanced version of EMS. It turned out our enhancements were tailor made for DESQview. It made their operating environment viable.

As a small company, they were more than willing to do whatever it took to work with us. They quickly modified their software and we cut a deal to bundle a copy of DESQview with every memory board we sold. That was no small matter. We were shipping well over 50,000 units per month.

This strategy gave us the software we needed to prove our spec was better. At the same time, bundling the software added value to our product. Quarterdeck went from obscurity to landing in the middle of the biggest battle in the industry.

We managed to out-flank Intel and stick it to Microsoft at the same time. Although there was never a question Windows and Microsoft would eventually triumph, it was still painful for Microsoft – and great fun for us – to see Quarterdeck thrive, even if it was for just a short time.

Microsoft put a lot of pressure on us to replace DESQview with Windows. They offered to support the EEMS spec and cut us a favorable deal for Windows. That is if we stopped doing business with Quarterdeck.

It is no accident Microsoft ended up in front of the Justice Department. During the initial stages of the DOJ's investigation I was questioned about this episode. Microsoft has been using suspect tactics for years. This was the first time I had witnessed it firsthand but it would not be the last. What they proposed may have very well crossed the border of ethics. It was a no-no and we didn't accept their offer. This pissed them off even more. We had a good laugh though.

The point of this story is we didn't sit idly by and surrender to a more powerful company. We shot back and shot back hard. Not only at them, but their partners too. Risky? Yes. Necessary? Yes. I haven't used a sports analogy for a while so now's a good time. Competing against a big company is what it must have been like to step into the boxing ring with Mike Tyson in his prime.

Tyson was a powerful puncher and imposing figure. His flaws were well hidden by his ability to intimidate his opponents. They didn't surface until someone who believed he could beat Tyson stepped in the ring with him. That someone was Buster Douglas, an opponent everyone considered nothing more than a tune-up fight for Tyson. Some tune-up.

Douglas knocked Tyson on his backside in Tokyo at a time when most fighters who fought Iron Mike lost before they even stepped into the ring. They were frightened by his reputation and petrified of being hurt.

That kind of attitude won't just get you beat in the boxing game. It will get you beat in the business game as well. You cannot afford to be intimidated by an opponent. Every person has flaws, and every company has flaws. Regardless of how powerful a company may appear, there are vulnerabilities. Find the weaknesses and exploit them to the extent possible.

That's what Buster Douglas did. Once he showed that Tyson could be beat, Tyson was never the same fighter. He had lost his psychological edge. Now he's considered just another bully with limited boxing skills.

So, back to the memory wars. We weren't intimidated. Maybe we were just too stupid to know better or maybe we realized we had our own set of advantages. We had demonstrated our technical expertise was every bit as good if not better than Intel's.

But striking back on the technical front was only half the battle. The next challenge was to demonstrate our marketing skills were up to the challenge. Other than Intel having more money and people, we weren't concerned about their ability to out-market us. We would negate their resource advantage by using the press.

The trade publications would be critical. Businesses relied on them to provide unbiased assessments of new technology, and key decision makers would be turning to the editorial community for opinions on the new memory standards. This was a battle we had to at least fight to a draw. It was a protracted effort, lasting more than a year. Nary a week went by where there wasn't some coverage about the standards and the war between Intel and my company.

It was a blast. Editors called for interviews constantly and they were always hoping for a little dirt. I wasn't bashful about speaking my mind and was more than happy to oblige. The press ate it up. It was a full-blown donnybrook. Maybe it wasn't the O.J. trial but in the technology biz it was about as exciting as it gets.

The press can be a very powerful vehicle in a company's marketing campaign. This is a major point. You don't need a big budget to compete effectively in the press. Editors don't discriminate against smaller organizations as long as the story is interesting.

Keep in mind, however, large companies do have some added leverage stemming from their large advertising budgets. Though there is a separation between the advertising side and editorial side, large companies are a substantial revenue source to publications. This can have a subtle indirect influence. For example, editors may not be as aggressive toward a big advertiser. That is not to say an editor will ever knowingly print something false, or overtly slant a story. They will not. But stories can be *softened* by the influence of advertising dollars.

The press is viewed as an unbiased source of information. Decision makers place more value on the information in an article than they do in what they read in an ad. This provides an opportunity for a small company to neutralize a larger company's advertising advantage. One favorable front-page article can be worth as much as hundreds of thousands of dollars in advertising. One reason is, favorable press can be used as on-going collateral in the form of reprints. This way, its value can be sustained over a longer period of time.

In using the press as a marketing tool there is one very important thing to remember: *never try to manufacture news.* This will be completely counterproductive. Editors understand the difference between news and propaganda. If you try to use the press to spout the company's sales pitch you will lose credibility.

Short of manufacturing news, when in a situation where the press has latched on to a story, you do need to try and milk it. To do that you have to give them more than the company line. Particularly for small companies, if all you tell the press is the same crap they get from your PR department, they will lose interest. On the other hand, if you ration out juicy comments and are willing to stick it to a competitor on the record, they'll keep coming back for more.

Don't be afraid to be a little provocative. Business publications are no different from daily newspapers and national magazines. They need to attract readers to make money. Their product is information, and trade and business press source a large part of that information from vendors. The more interesting and controversial it is, the better.

I wasn't shy and I had no love for Intel. It came naturally to me to accommodate the press. So much so that at one point I was censured for something I had said. I don't even remember what it was, but I recall it wasn't a good thing. Naturally, I didn't think it was a big deal. You know the old saying, *any press is good press.* The problem was, my management didn't subscribe to that notion.

My hiatus didn't last very long. When management realized

they weren't getting coverage the gag quickly came off. Editors knew me and trusted me. They wanted to talk to the people in charge. And they wanted to talk with people who gave them interesting things to write.

I was sitting on top of all of this and had developed a rapport with the key editors. With me not talking there was no one to fill the void. Management decided I had been punished enough and I was again permitted to talk to the press. At first I was required to be supervised. That lasted about a week. After that I was free to do what was necessary to get coverage.

One more point on the press. *Business is about cultivating relationships and the press is no exception.* Even when you don't have anything in particular to talk about you should maintain contact with key editors. This can be done by phone or at industry events like trade shows. Don't be afraid to call them for an opinion or to ask them if they've heard anything interesting. Just make sure you don't call on deadline day. The best time to call is the day after their deadlines.

At industry events, publications often sponsor hospitality suites or promotional gatherings. Attend them and make the rounds. Doing so will help lay the groundwork for future coverage. It also helps ensure they'll call for a quote for general articles published in your market.

When it was all said and done, we had weathered the storm. That's not to say Intel hadn't established itself in the business. They had. However, we managed to hold our own with the new memory technology. More importantly, we held on to our existing revenue stream. I later became friends with my counterpart at Intel. After many years when the events and technology were but a distant memory, we shared our sales numbers. It turns out we pretty much split the market 50/50. That wasn't bad considering the hole we started in.

So you see, a small company can effectively battle a big one. We didn't try to outspend them. We could not have succeeded just as Buster Douglas could not have out-punched Mike Tyson. We used the press to level the playing field in the same way Douglas used his jab to avoid getting hit and to wear down his opponent. We took an aggressive stance by improving Intel's technology. Buster Douglas ignored Tyson's reputation and took the fight to Tyson. Douglas was something like an 80 to 1 underdog. We had to battle three of the biggest companies in the industry. We both not only survived, but thrived.

PART II

This second tale serves to show it was no fluke our tactics worked. My hope is, this will enhance your confidence that the strategy has a broad application and the positive outcomes were not merely isolated incidents.

The second run in with Goliath was also against Intel. This time they had no partners. But we were dealing with a second mega competitor - AT&T. The battleground was desktop videoconferencing. As mentioned earlier, I was heading the marketing effort for the industry leader. Shortly after we announced our first desktop product, Intel entered the market with a similar product.

It wasn't so much Intel wanted to get in the videoconferencing business. They had other motives. Their goal was to create demand for a CPU-intensive application. This would, in turn, give people a reason to buy PCs featuring their high-end Pentium processor. CPU stands for central processing unit and is considered the brain of the PC. Faster and more powerful processors are more expensive and more profitable. Since selling processors was Intel's main business, their strategy made sense.

The Pentium was Intel's top-of-the-line CPU and they were

focused on encouraging people to buy it. To accomplish that, they created a software-based videoconferencing product. When it comes to using CPU power, video is off the charts. Videoconferencing requires the picture to be constantly updated. Good video requires at least 15 frames per second (fps). TV-quality video requires between 24 and 30 fps. Even with a CPU as powerful as the Pentium, quality video is tough to pull off in software. That didn't matter to Intel. They were not concerned with producing the highest quality video. They just wanted to create demand for video to enhance the sales of Pentiums.

AT&T also had ulterior motives. As a telecom company, AT&T was interested in selling bandwidth. They wanted people to spend more time using expensive telephone lines. Video was the perfect application. To get even 15 fps you needed an ISDN line. ISDN is a high-speed line capable of handling 128kps or more of data. At best, a standard phone line can get 56kps. Even with 128kps, video quality is marginal. But it was good enough for a segment of the business market. And it served AT&T's desire to sell more network-usage minutes.

Here we were, a $250 million company up against two multi-billion dollar companies who were household names. Making matters worse, no one in the PC industry knew who we were. My company had been selling big conference room systems to the telecommunications side of corporations. Up to the point we introduced our first PC product, no one in the PC industry had heard of us. To top it off, Intel was selling their product for a couple of thousand dollars while ours cost six thousand dollars.

Let's recap. One little company was up against two very big companies. One little company nobody knew was facing off against two big companies everyone knew. One little company had a very expensive product while the two big companies had much less expensive products. Time to surrender right? Are you kidding? Come on Intel, we wanna kick you in – uhhh, your other shin – now.

It couldn't get any better as far as I was concerned. I still hated Intel, and kicking the crap out of AT&T would be a piece of cake. AT&T was of little concern. Telecommunications companies always struggled to compete in the PC market. After years of enjoying the fruits of a monopoly there weren't many managers in senior positions at AT&T who really knew how to compete.

Sure, they were big and had lots of resources. But they were also slow and bureaucratic and would give up as soon as things got tough. Even if you believed the most optimistic projections for videoconferencing, the market wasn't attractive enough for a company the size of AT&T. Eventually they would leave it to others to create demand for their higher-end services.

It came down to Intel and us. In actuality, Intel's decision to enter the market was a good thing. Videoconferencing was a fledgling market and we were a *nobody*. The moment Intel entered the fray the spotlight was on the technology and us. It gave credibility to the market and brought more attention than we could have ever achieved on our own. It was a double-edged sword, but all in all, I considered it a positive.

I can't say management viewed it that way. They did their typical sky is falling routine. Our CEO was even quoted in BusinessWeek saying he didn't know how we would compete. Way to go management. Nothing like encouraging the troops! Luckily I didn't care a lick whether or not management thought we could compete. Fortunately, as a start-up division, we were given a great deal of latitude to do what we felt was best.

The scenario played out much like the first battle against Intel. They used FUD to try to convince potential buyers we were a shaky company that might not be around for the long haul. Adding insult to injury, to seed the market they were practically giving their product away.

This is a common tactic for larger companies. The Japanese used it successfully for years to penetrate the U.S. market. We didn't have that luxury. We needed the money. Our product wasn't expensive because we were gouging our customers. It was expensive because the damn thing cost an arm and a leg to build. Remember, we had taken technology from $25,000 systems to use on the PC.

The mantra was still aggressiveness. We had to take advantage of the spotlight Intel had placed on the market. We needed to formulate a strategy to negate Intel's price advantage and limit the damage being done by their product give away. At the same time, we could not totally ignore AT&T.

We had one thing going for us. Our product was head and shoulders above the rest in quality. Better yet, we knew from experience there was a minimum quality threshold for videoconferencing products to be accepted by the corporate market. If you went below it, it didn't really matter what the product cost, or even if you gave it away. Intel, being new to the business did not realize that fact.

The campaign we devised was a head-to-head comparison of our respective products. We called it the Main Event and used a boxing motif as the backdrop. The theory was to *knock out the competition* by showing the market our product superiority. Sports sometimes has a practical application in business.

The campaign consisted of an eight-city tour. We would have liked more, but that was all our budget would allow. We lined our product up side by side with Intel's and AT&T's and proceeded to show why the competition could not hold a candle to us. Our goal was to convince buyers the competitors' products would be virtually useless as a communications tool.

The gloves were off and the campaign worked to perfection. We not only demonstrated our superiority, we also leveled the playing field in terms of company stature. This was a byproduct of our willingness to make a direct product comparison and crafting and articulating a message based on years of experience in the field. Intel and AT&T were learning the business. Their resources were no substitute for experience. That was their weakness. Like guerilla warfare, we had the advantage of knowing the battleground. Hit and retreat and use your territorial knowledge to your advantage.

This is a key point. *When a company, large or small, gets into a new market they will be at a disadvantage to an incumbent.* No matter how much research a company might conduct before entering a market, they won't be able to identify every nuance. Incumbents have a territorial advantage and need to closely examine the new entrant's product and strategy to find the flaws caused by their lack of experience.

Our Main Event strategy also resonated with the press. Just as before, the media loved a good fight and we were giving them one. This upstart company had the nerve to go right after Intel. What they didn't realize is, it wasn't so much a matter of nerve as it was survival. In my mind, we didn't have many choices. We had to aggressively counter their name recognition and price advantage or we would be squashed. Taking pot shots at Intel in the process didn't hurt either. We didn't shy away from engaging Intel in a battle of words, but we never used dirty tricks. Our attacks were always product related.

The media again played a critical role in achieving our marketing objectives. This time they gave us equal footing in the market and helped create name and brand recognition. We received exposure our advertising budget couldn't afford to pay for.

This is important to note. When competing against a large recognized company, a good marketing tactic is to *try to provoke a fight*. As the little guy, try to get the bigger company to acknowledge your presence. This serves to elevate you to their level. When articles are published mentioning both companies you begin to look like you belong. This can often create instant credibility in the eyes of the reader.

Most people never see the companies they do business with. They have no way of knowing whether you're big or small unless they take the time to investigate. The press is a powerful tool in combating larger companies as long as you can find an angle attractive to them.

In both case we had that angle and we executed an aggressive *in your face* counter attack. The press will always play a crucial role in these situations. They can compensate for the difference in advertising and general media budgets as long as the story is interesting. Remember, small companies cannot and should not ever attempt to manufacture news. The media frowns on it and any attempt to do so will backfire. It will cost you when you have something truly newsworthy to talk about. But if the opportunity presents itself, take it and stay aggressive. And, it's worth saying again, don't just mouth the party line if you hope to sustain interest with editors.

Executing an aggressive marketing campaign depends largely upon the ability to demonstrate some clear product advantage. If you possess an advantage or can quickly develop one, you should not hesitate to aggressively promote it. Being passive when faced with superior forces is a recipe for defeat. If you're going to go down, go down fighting.

In both cases the necessary elements existed and we were able to succeed. In the latter case we established ourselves as the industry leader in PC videoconferencing. AT&T eventually dropped out and, even better, they started reselling our product. We succeeded when few gave us much of a chance. We kicked Goliath in the uhh...shins again and lived to tell about it.

Got Music?

Not long ago, a science brief published in the Boston Globe discussed the effect of music on animals. Apparently cows produce more milk when listening to the soothing sounds of Beethoven. I acquired a newfound respect for chickens, as they seem to like Pink Floyd. I'll think more fondly of the next chicken I dine on.

Over the years, much has also been written about the impact of music on child development. Whether any of this is hard science is unclear. Logic dictates people exposed to a range of artistic, cultural, and intellectual pursuits are more likely to be well rounded and more accomplished human beings. A breadth of knowledge and experience can nourish the ability to understand the many facets of human nature. But discounting the possibility music may make you smarter, why is it relevant?

Answering this requires a brief explanation of the dual aspects of marketing: product management and product marketing. The dividing line between the two occurs at the point a product is ready for market.

Generally, product management is responsible for defining product plans and working with product development to implement those plans. As the product nears the launch phase, responsibilities transition to product marketing. Product marketing, in turn, manages the marketing communications tasks such as advertising, public relations, and the creation of collateral. These two aspects of marketing require different skills. It is the area of product marketing where an artistic flair plays a major role.

Developing an advertising campaign is not unlike writing a

book or making a movie. The goal is to tell a story. Advertising's story is a product message. Ads may include some *entertainment value* to help convey the message. But the entertainment component should always be secondary to the product message. The primary goal of a book or movie may be to entertain while a secondary goal could be to communicate a more meaningful message. The priorities may differ but the parallels exist.

Creating TV and print ads, multimedia Web messaging, collateral, and even an effective company logo all require a general sense of aesthetics. Not that you need the skill to actually develop the artistic component. Illustrators, graphic artists, and copywriters specialize in the creation process. But product marketing has to recognize what works and what doesn't. They also must balance the desires of these graphic specialists to create *great art* against the need to effectively communicate the product message. For that, an artistic eye is essential.

When I started in marketing, technology companies had yet to create this division in marketing. A product manager had *cradle to grave* responsibility. This meant the same person who developed the product ideas also brought the product to market, and handled the end-of-life (EOL) issues. As businesses migrated toward specialization, it became increasingly rare for a single person to possess the range of skills necessary to see a product through its entire life cycle.

I was fortunate to have cut my teeth in marketing before specialization was in vogue. It allowed me to develop a complete set of skills. These skills serve to separate me from many of today's marketing professionals. If I were to use a sports analogy, and of course I will, it would be like a boxer with power in both hands, a baseball player who hits for average and has power, or a basketball player who can score and play defense. Athletes like these are rare. So are marketing people who can handle both product marketing and product management.

Damn, it's another commercial. You had been warned that you were not finished having to deal with these attempts to impress. Come on, it's really not so bad. We deal with commercials in every walk of life – TV, radio, driving down the interstate, on the Internet, at airports, in magazines. Let's face it, that's the way business works. Where there are people (here again, that would be you) there will be some company or uhh writer (me again) plugging its goods and services. Why not in a book? The good part of putting a commercial in a book is you can hit the head and not miss the commercial. Well not good for you but good for me.

Fasten your seatbelts and make sure your trays are in the upright and locked position; Shameless Self-Promotion II just ahead.

The heart of business focuses on a sampling of marketing principles, many of which are related to marketing communications activities. Issues like branding, public relations, product messaging and positioning, and the effective use of the Internet.

Why am I qualified to discuss these issues? Partly because of experience. When you manage every facet of marketing for over two decades something has to rub off. Part of it is also because I take pride in possessing a diverse set of interests, knowledge, and experiences. Early in life, I was exposed to a wealth of artistic and cultural stimuli. And not the MTV variety. No, it wasn't from watching TV or listening to the radio, it was from doing and seeing firsthand.

My parents, like most parents, encouraged me to play a musical instrument. Even at the age of eight I demonstrated an understanding of theoretical probabilities by selecting the violin. It wasn't because of any particular love for the violin. It was because my chances of making the orchestra were greater.

Most kids chose more popular instruments. I decided to go after a niche market and lessen the competition. I sensed early my talents didn't lie in the area of music and wanted to increase my chance of success. You have to know your weaknesses and pick your shots. Later, I did migrate to more popular instruments including the trumpet, piano, and briefly the guitar.

As a kid I became fairly accomplished with the trumpet and violin. This provided experience in both classical music and jazz. Don't get me wrong; no one except my parents was ever going to pay a plug nickel to hear me play. On the contrary, people were more likely to pay for me to stop playing.

Like most kids, I eventually gave up music. I hated practicing and lacked the passion for playing. But the experience provided a foundation to appreciate and understand the aesthetic world. This would prove valuable for the profession I ultimately chose.

Building on this musical experience, and without any parental prodding, I began to pursue a wide range of cultural interests. This involved experiencing, in person, an array of the very best musicians, performers, and artists in the world – everything from hard rock, to jazz, classical, ballet, modern dance, and a range of theatre and performance art. The goal was simple. Seek out the best in the world, experience their talents, and try to understand the particular *beauty* each had to offer.

The list of has grown quite large and includes some of the greatest performers to ever grace this planet. A sampling includes: Led Zeppelin, The Stones, Miles Davis, Sting, Eric Clapton, The Who, B.B King, Ray Charles, Sade, Alan Alda, Nathan Lane, Lauren Bacall, Robert Klein, Stockard Channing, John Lithgow, Leonard Bernstein, Mikhail Baryshnikov,

Marcel Marceau, even Frank Sinatra.

I actually saw Sinatra twice. Once with Dean Martin and once solo. I confess, left to my own devices, I wouldn't have ever seen Sinatra but I'm glad I did. My ex-father-in-law was the person who supplied the tickets. He was a big fan. He was also a small time bookie back in New York and let's just say he had ticket *connections* if you get my drift.

Eventually, I augmented my musical and theatrical interests with a deep appreciation for art. This appreciation ranges from classic representational art, to the impressionists, to surrealism. Although the catalyst was an attempt to impress a woman, art has taken its place alongside business and sports as one of my greatest passions. In this case it may be because of a complete lack of talent as I have trouble drawing stick figures. But there are few things I find more fascinating than beautiful works of art.

In our travels, my better half and I have frequented the world's finest museums and galleries and stood in awe of the some of the most famous works ever produced – Rembrandt's Mona Lisa, Da Vinci's Last Supper, Michel Angelo's David as well as the Sistine Chapel, Van Gough's Starry Nights, Degas, Monet, Dali, Gauguin, and on and on. The art and artists we have seen would fill many pages. We are also proud to have assembled a collection of what we hope are some of today's emerging artists.

Now, you have to admit, there aren't many people, particularly sports fans with that range of experience. Might make for a well-rounded person don't you think? When combined with an extensive background in marketing it just might equip a person to recognize an effective ad or brochure if they saw one too.

PART THREE · THE MIND

CHAPTER TEN

Where Egos Fly

To some, it may be hard to believe companies can be significantly impacted by the egos of management. Particularly in public companies where stockholders and the board of directors theoretically serve to temper such behavior. Here is some insight. In most public companies the board spends very little time being involved in the business. Under normal circumstances they meet once a quarter. Often, these meetings consist of nothing more than patting the management team on their collective asses.

The board and the management team are all members of the same club. There really isn't much in the way of checks and balances. Serving on a board is prestigious. Board members are paid a stipend and often get enough stock in the company to make it extremely worthwhile. It's not in the board's interest to challenge management unless forced by events such as mounting financial losses. That being the case, it's not far fetched to think ego can inject itself into the decision-making process.

The technology industry is replete with high-profile examples of such misbehavior. And I doubt high tech is unique. Take, for instance, the hatred between Scott McNealy, the founder and chairman of Sun Microsystems and Bill Gates. Do you think the decision to develop Java was solely based on sound business judgment? Or, perhaps, did it have something to do with McNealy wanting to stick it to Gates because he thought Bill was getting a bit too big for his britches?

Java is touted as an alternative development platform and operating environment to Microsoft Windows. The technology has technical merit and has gained a foothold in the Internet space. But it is unclear whether Sun will ever recoup the massive investment it has made in the technology.

There's also no love lost between Larry Ellison, the CEO of Oracle, and Gates. Ellison once admitted using private investigators to literally dig up dirt on Microsoft. Ellison was trying to aid the Justice Department's antitrust case against Microsoft. Allegedly, a $1,200 offer was made to janitors to get a look at the garbage of a trade group allied with Microsoft. I'm sure Mr. Ellison only had the best interests of the country in mind.

These are industry heavyweights running multi-billion companies. Despite that, they often act like spoiled children who can't play in the same sandbox without fighting. So it should not be surprising this kind of misbehavior permeates the business world.

Though not surprising, it is disheartening to think about how many critical business decisions are made to satisfy the egos of management. Everything from company acquisitions, to sponsoring high-profile sporting events, to plunking down millions of dollars to buy stadium-naming rights are often done for the wrong reasons.

We once placed a full-page ad in the Wall Street Journal at a cost of $186,000 simply because of ego. This was a huge amount of money for the company and we only had the budget to run the one ad. Anyone who has taken even the most basic marketing course knows placing a single ad in a publication is like burning money. Particularly in a daily newspaper, even if it is the Journal. But there was cachet with advertising in the Journal. The founders wanted to do it, so we did.

My first exposure to the effects of ego occurred when working for the PC enhancement board company mentioned in the *David and Goliath* chapter. My time with this company was the best experience of my career. The industry was emerging and the company was at the heart of the revolution. The company was relatively large but the founders maintained an entrepreneurial spirit. They allowed people to make decisions and didn't bog the process down with bureaucracy. We had the best of both worlds, the resources of a larger company and the agility of a start-up.

Despite our success, the founders were not satisfied. At the time, the truly elite companies were those actually producing the PCs. The top companies were not much different than today and included IBM, Apple, Compaq, and Dell. There were also countless smaller companies trying to get in on the action. If anything, the market was already overcrowded. There wasn't a supply problem or any particular need for more PC manufacturers; however when there is money to be made, there is never a lack of companies eager to take a shot.

Microsoft and a handful of application software companies were becoming major forces, but the focus was on the hardware platform. The big PC players were leading the way. The executives at these companies were held in the highest regard. Although our company was a recognized name, the founders did not command the respect or attention of their PC counterparts.

What to do about it? Make PCs. We already made many of the components that went into the PC, so how hard could it be to make the whole damn thing? A lot harder than we thought. But that's a story for another day.

As expected, the proper spin was put on the decision to enter this new and highly competitive market. There was the fear our enhancement business would decline as PC vendors built more powerful and feature-rich PCs. There was also the issue of eroding margins and the fact that the market was heading toward commodity status. All legitimate, but premature concerns. It would be years before these issues would surface.

The only reason that was remotely valid for the decision was the feeling we could not achieve the magic billion-dollar mark by staying where we were. This, as it turned out, was not accurate, but it was reasonable thinking for the time.

Even if you agreed we couldn't get to a billion in revenues, was that a valid reason to take such a risky move years before any such move was necessary? Wouldn't it have been more appropriate to stay the course, secure our market leading position, and see what opportunities presented themselves? Wouldn't it have been better to wait for something more consistent with our core competencies? No, the overriding reason we entered the PC market was ego.

Many of us, including yours truly, thought it was a terrible idea. We had a solid, growing, profitable business. We were number one in our market. Why put it in jeopardy for such a high-risk venture? There were better and far less risky ways to ensure our growth and profitability for many years to come. As a consequence, initially I wanted no part of the new business. That soon changed.

It was fascinating to watch the internal process. The company decided to start a new business unit. Now it had to staff it. The good news was that the founders, along with a few key engineers, were handling all the early heavy lifting. The founders were bright and had complementary skills. One was your classic engineering/operations guy, another – by far the brightest of the three – was the strategic thinker and driving force behind the marketing effort, and the last one's claim to fame was he spoke English better than the other two and handled all the external affairs of the company. A dubious skill, but it was important to the company's success at the time.

The core group was more than capable of defining the initial product. The problem was no one was in place to take the ball and run with it. All the key aspects of the business unit needed to be addressed – product management, sales, support and operations.

Logic suggests an endeavor this important calls for your best people. Unfortunately, this wasn't a scientific endeavor, it was business, and logic doesn't always apply. The fact was the best people didn't want any part of this folly. Most of us thought it was going to be a resounding failure. To the founder's credit, they didn't force anyone to participate. To their discredit, I don't believe they provided any incentives for anyone to take the risk.

What they did was classic Rube Goldberg. They went around and asked department heads for the names of people they would be willing to give up to the new group. My god. We had an expansion draft going on! An expansion draft is where new teams get to select players from existing teams. The catch is the existing teams get to protect their best players. This leaves only the less skilled players available for the new team.

The net effect is expansion teams are usually terrible. They often end up in last place for the first few years. It works in the sports industry because fans (the customers) understand and accept that this is how it works. Cities hungry for a major-league team live through the lean times with the hope management will be smart enough to create a contender down the line.

In the business world, especially high tech, no such luxury is afforded the teams. Mostly, you get one shot and you better make it good. The thought of staffing such an important effort with everyone's cast-offs was chilling to say the least. It certainly heightened my level of concern about the viability of the project. But it wasn't my problem. Not yet anyway.

Watching from a distance was more than a bit surreal. A good friend and colleague of mine would joke about the keystone cops-like nature of the effort. From top to bottom the new unit was staffed with misfits and lightweights. The chances for success were diminishing by the day. That's when my friend and I decided we needed to at least make an attempt to assist. This wasn't a charitable act. We were concerned the entire company could be brought down if this thing didn't at least tread water.

We formed a team and started providing our input to the founders. Our only intention was to try to ensure all the basic stuff was covered and a reasonable plan was in place. No one in the new group had the slightest idea how to go about forming a new business. This continued for a while and we were becoming more comfortable with the new venture when one day, one of the founders called me into his office. He made an offer I couldn't refuse.

How would I like to take over the PC business unit? His confidence in me was flattering, but I still had concerns about our ability to pull it off. The market was cutthroat, even back then. We didn't have the necessary infrastructure to adequately support the product, nor did we really know how to build quality PCs. We had the engineering talent to design a competitive product, but that wasn't enough. We had to re-brand and reposition the company and retool our distribution channels. It would take a lot of money and time. Time we did not have. The planned launch was less than six months away.

Saying yes had more to do with ego than good business judgment. I still thought the whole thing was a long shot. Arrogantly, I felt if anyone in the company was capable of pulling it off I was the guy. Oh, I know, I'm awash in modesty. I can tell you without a doubt, regardless of whom you talk to, no one has ever accused me of being modest. Love or hate me, that's one thing everyone agrees on. I can be an arrogant S.O.B. Being a marketing person, my spin would be that I possess supreme confidence in my ability. That sounds better than being a conceited prick. Yeah, I think we'll go with that – supreme confidence.

I took the job and my friend joined me. We were a good team. I would focus on the tactical and business side and he would focus on the technical and strategic aspects of the business. We tried to keep expectations low. We didn't want people getting overly optimistic. That, as we discussed earlier, can be deadly. Besides, it worked for George W. and if it's good enough for the President of the United States it's good enough for me. Our initial forecast was for somewhere between 5,000 and 10,000 units per month. A trivial number today, but a challenge back then.

Having taken the assignment, I had to decide where to start. That wasn't difficult. I have a technique when taking on new assignments: first, assess the team. Everything starts with the people. You have to ensure you have the right mix of talent. You also need to make sure the people you have are in the best position to leverage their individual skill sets. This point is very important.

Regardless of the situation, most of the people either working with or for you, are going to be average. Many aspects of life can be analyzed using the tried and true *bell curve*. It certainly applies to people. Most of the world is in the middle of the curve with superstars and incompetents being on the edges. Obviously you want to attract as many superstars and eliminate as many incompetents as possible.

I recently read an article about Jack Welch, the celebrated CEO of General Electric who espoused a similar philosophy. GE managers were instructed to categorize people by A, B, and C. The As, or superstars, get promotions and raises; the Bs, average people; do well; and the Cs, incompetents, get fired. Sounds basic right? It is rarely done.

By definition, superstars are hard to come by. They will invariably make up the minority of any team. The trick to putting a good team together is understanding and accepting the fact that most people are average. The challenge is to make the most of what they can offer.

Most average people excel at some task. Perhaps it's because they have a natural affinity for it, or perhaps it's because they enjoy doing a specific function. In the interview process try to assess the particular talent a person possesses and see if you can put them in a role which will maximize that talent. With a handful of superstars and a group of average people who like what they're doing, you can go a long way.

Once the team is in place, responsibilities need to be defined. Further, goals, expectations, and objectives need to be communicated. You need to make sure everyone is on the same page. After this is in place, then worry about the product and marketing plan. A plan is not worth the paper it's printed on if you don't have the ability to execute it. That takes people. My advice is to always start with the people.

Speaking of people, when last we left the Caped Crusaders they had just inherited the '62 Mets. The '62 Mets were one of those expansion teams and will go down in history as one of the worst baseball teams ever assembled. Their season record was an abysmal 40 wins and 120 losses and they finished a whopping 60 1/2 games out of first place. That gives you an idea of just how bad things were for this new venture.

My amusement at the process that created this new team quickly turned to angst. You see, the bell curve had been skewed and the normal percentage of incompetent people had swelled to biblical proportions. OK. Maybe not biblical proportions but it wasn't pretty. What to do, what to do?

Easy, it was slash and burn time. This wasn't a day care center. Time was short and there was too much to be done to try and mold this group of misfits into a cohesive team. Part of me felt like firing or transferring the lot of them, but that wasn't practical. I needed bodies and it would take time to recruit new people. We had to live with what we had. Fortunately, there were some good people. Certainly some people who were competent enough to make a positive contribution. There just weren't enough of them.

Needless to say I didn't make many friends. People were

moved around. It was also made clear that whatever anyone else had promised them regarding a potential new career path didn't apply anymore. They would be judged solely on their ability to perform their newly assigned responsibilities.

There were some amusing conversations during this process. How would you like to find out some of your so-called product managers had not only never seen a marketing requirements document (MRD), but didn't even know what one was? And no one in the group was even aware of our business goals. Business plan, what business plan? Sales objectives, what sales objectives?

On top of all of this, the two people I replaced as division head were none too happy and one of them was now working for me. I had known her for quite some time, dating back to my first corporate job. She and I never hit it off, even before this gig.

Better yet, like a real-world soap opera it turns out she was romantically involved with the other former department head. Great, a two-for-one sale. If one of them missed stabbing me in the back the other one would nail me on the rebound. It's funny now and I hold no ill will toward these people. They ended up getting married and living happily ever after, as far as I know. I'm not exactly on their Christmas card list.

Where were we? Oh, yes. I had a team of unhappy campers. But I was young and brash and I didn't lose any sleep over it. If they weren't happy they were free to leave. You know, don't let the door hit you in the ass on the way out. I had bigger problems. With a series of stopgap adjustments the team would do for now. My partner and I would fill in the holes and we would solicit support from the rest of the organization.

Now we needed a strategy. And we needed to make sure the other organizations in the company were properly positioned to support our efforts. We quickly put together a business plan and product strategy. It was based on some existing work but was mostly the creation of my colleague and myself. It wasn't nuclear physics. Anyone with half a brain knew what had to be done. There were some subtleties, but it was more a matter of executing the fundamentals, like developing realistic sales, revenue, and profit targets. We completed it all, including the reorganization, within 90 days.

Our confidence was increasing with every passing day. We still had significant problems, but their number and severity were diminishing.

Then the proverbial other shoe dropped. Or should I say guillotine. One day I get back from lunch and my secretary (yes they were still called secretaries back then) tells me my boss (one of the founders) wants to see me right away. OK, no big deal, we got together all the time, nothing out of the ordinary here.

That is until my colleague says to me, "We're out of here." I asked him, "What do you mean, *we're out of here*?" He tells me they're pulling the group from us. Translation: they're pulling the group from me. I couldn't believe it. Why would they do that? How could they do that! But sure enough I go to the boss' office and before I could even sit down, the words flew out of his mouth like daggers. "Tony, you've got a morale problem and you've acted unprofessionally. You have two choices, go back and run the board division or quit." I was stunned.

Naturally, my first reaction was to discuss the matter. Unbelievably, he did not give me a chance to defend myself. Nor were the issues ever fully explained. I knew there was a morale problem. That was a non-issue, at least from the perspective of getting the job done. The people who were unhappy were the same people who were not qualified to be there in the first place. I had not concerned myself with their hurt feelings. We had a business to run, and even if you concede it was an issue, how can such a drastic decision be made without at least giving me an opportunity to correct the situation?

What bothered me most was the comment about my professionalism. I never really found out what he meant by that. I had my suspicions, but never pursued it. Whatever it was could not have been terribly egregious since they were offering me the opportunity to go back to my old job and be responsible for the majority of the company's revenue. In any case, it was over.

What can be learned from this experience? What did I do wrong and how can the impact of ego be minimized? Let me tackle what I did wrong first because I have an answer for that question.

The primary error I made was not managing up. My focus was totally on what needed to be done below me. I was not concerned with my boss or what his expectations may have been. That, I believe, was the real reason behind my demise.

What I should have considered, but was too young and inexperienced to realize, was my boss wanted and needed to be involved in the process. Although I kept him informed and consulted him on all the major decisions, I was basically working autonomously. When I needed help I would ask for it. Other than that, we were busy running the day-to-day operations.

It was the same thing I did when I joined the company. I just kept on doing it with the new group. Only this time there was a dramatic difference. When I came into the company the founder was mentally prepared to give up control of the board group. He was tired of running it and was looking for new challenges. It was a different story with the PC group. This was his baby. He didn't want to be cut out of the deal. He wanted to be integrally involved and I didn't make that happen.

I needed to do a better job of taking care of my boss' needs. That didn't mean relying on him to make decisions. In this case it meant making him feel part of the process. I should have asked his opinion and bounced ideas, big and small, off of him.

I should have asked for advice even if I didn't need it. I should have made him feel needed.

This was not about kissing the boss' butt. That was not the case. Nor would you ever hear me recommend doing that under any circumstances. It was about ensuring that the person who had the ultimate decision-making power and who had conceived of the idea in the first place continued to be part of the process.

Did I need to do any of those things to perform my job or to be successful? No, probably not. I just needed to do them to keep the boss happy. A painful lesson to say the least. Business is not just about developing and executing marketing strategies. In a management role, it's mostly about managing people, and that includes those who work for you and those you work for.

Another lesson that came from this was a recognition that sometimes you can move too quickly. To this day I would argue this particular situation warranted quick action, but what I did was drastic. No one was prepared for my actions, and this created enemies instead of allies. Although every decision was sound, it was a case of too much, too quickly.

Additionally, I failed to recognize the larger political and cultural issues. Many of the people who were upset were long-time employees. Many were with the company in the early stages. We may have been a $300 million company but there was still an entrepreneurial atmosphere and an open-door policy. Anyone could walk into the office of one of the founders and discuss any issue. Evidently someone did.

Experience would have allowed me to recognize these conditions. If I had seen the *big picture* I could have altered the pace of change. If that was inappropriate, I could have preempted any complaints by going to my boss first to discuss my intentions and their potential results. Then, when people complained, I would have had the buy-in of my superior.

How did this end up? Since patience isn't one of my greatest virtues and I have zero tolerance for being mistreated, I made up my mind within seconds to leave the company. I didn't make the official decision immediately. I was advised to cool off and think about it. You don't want to make an important decision when you're upset. I was offered the opportunity to take a couple of weeks off at the company's expense and think about what I wanted to do.

I mean, it wasn't like I would be sweeping the floor. I was offered the opportunity to continue in my previous capacity. The job was arguably the second most important marketing position in the company, and there were many people who respected me and wanted me to stay. All in all, a pretty good consolation prize.

But it didn't matter. The damage was done. It wasn't so much the blow to my ego as it was the way the matter was handled. Under no circumstances should I – or anyone else – have been treated like that. Everyone deserves an opportunity to fix whatever problems may exist. At the very least I deserved the opportunity to state my side of the story. I didn't do that to anyone in the group. Despite being certain many of them had no chance to succeed, they all had a chance to prove me wrong. This was clearly something I could not forgive.

At the end of the two weeks I respectfully resigned my position at the company, a company I thoroughly enjoyed working for. I gave up one of the most prestigious positions in the industry because of an unbending principle that I would never allow myself to be treated unfairly. One could argue principle had nothing to do with it. That it was all about ego. I won't deny ego was a factor. But it was a distant second to not having been given a fair shake.

Hell, if it were about ego I would have stayed around. Things changed so fast in the company that I probably could have worked my way back into the PC position after paying the appropriate penance. I was still the most talented marketing executive in the company.

I just couldn't bring myself to do it. That chapter in my life was over. It was time to move on. That decision, more than any other in the course of my career, led me to this point. It was an epiphany of sorts. I realized for the first time there were things I would not do for money or to achieve my professional goals.

What happened to the company and the PC effort? The previous department heads were reinstated, which meant the founders would be running the show. In April of that year, two months before the launch of our PC, IBM committed one of the worst mistakes ever committed in the industry. In their arrogance, they thought they could still dictate terms to the market. Hell, they were IBM. Whatever they said corporate America would follow. Not!

What did IBM do? They introduced a version of the PC called the PS/2® with a new architecture called MicroChannel®. For those of you who weren't there, MicroChannel was a pseudo-proprietary bus architecture. All PCs up to that point were AT class machines with an ISA bus. Why was that important? The bus inside the PC is where all the add-on cards and incremental functionality are plugged in. By changing the bus you also change all the cards that plug into the bus. And IBM was the only company with the design for the new MicroChannel bus. That meant IBM had a great deal of control. At least they thought they did.

What IBM had instead was a huge blunder and a rapidly declining market share. The days of doing whatever *Big Blue* said were over. This wasn't the mainframe business, but

IBM still had a mainframe mentality. The market, and in particular the business community, was perfectly happy with the old PCs. In fact, they preferred them. They worked fine and they knew how to support them.

The MicroChannel PC did not possess any significant new functionality but it would be completely different from a support standpoint. Plus, IBM would have more control over everyone's destiny. IBM compounded their mistake by shutting down production of their own AT machines. All they would offer from that point forward were MicroChannel-based PCs.

Yet again, another example of the *I'd rather be lucky than good* cliché in action. Given that IBM was a market leader at the time, when they stopped making the AT class ISA bus machines, the market started scrambling in search of anyone who could deliver one.

All of a sudden every little PC manufacturer had a windfall. If they could make PCs with an ISA bus, they could sell them. That included my former company. As it turned out, the company's forecast was wrong. They were selling 20,000 PCs a month right out of the gate. They couldn't build them fast enough. The fact they couldn't get them to work reliably when they did build them didn't even matter. Customers put up with the problems and a new PC company was born.

The company eventually became a fairly substantial player in the PC market. They did achieve their goal of $1 billion revenues. They went on to acquire the Tandy division from Radio Shack and ultimately grew to almost $2 billion before falling from the sky. They eventually crashed and burned after my former boss was ousted in a power struggle. This left them with an intellectual void from which the company never recovered.

I still keep in touch with my ex-boss. We get together every now and then when I'm in California and his schedule permits.

After years of wondering, I asked him if he harbored any hard feelings about the way I left the company. Not surprising, he couldn't even recall the circumstances. The entire affair might have been a big deal in my life, but it was just a minor blip in his. Talk about a bruise to one's ego.

I've been avoiding addressing the issue of ego. If there is an answer to the question of ego I don't presume to know what it is. Addressing ego's role in business is problematic. I don't believe ego or other innate human traits can ever be fully eliminated from daily business life. On the contrary, when you consider the size of a person's ego is often directly proportional to the level of their success, ego is not likely to disappear from the ranks of management any time soon.

I can only suggest when facing any decision, try and check your ego at the door. Stay objective. Ego and emotion only cloud a person's judgment. And won't your ego ultimately benefit more by continually making sound business decisions? Isn't that the best way to avoid mistakes and achieve long-term success?

I do know if you find yourself in a company where the CEO or founder's ego is out of control, be very wary. No good can come from this. Not only does an overblown ego taint the decision-making process but it also tends to prevent anyone else's opinion from being heard. Invariably, every decision will be driven by such an egomaniac.

Having said that, my ego wouldn't be satisfied if I didn't tell you the strategy we authored for the PC division was successfully executed, and the people I wanted to get rid of all left or were reassigned in a fairly short period of time. So, for having given up the opportunity to be a major player at one of the top companies in the industry at least I have the comfort of knowing that I was right after all. That and a buck will get me on a bus.

CHAPTER ELEVEN

Accentuate the Negative

This is not the most intuitive concept to follow but once you consider the logic, it becomes evident it is an effective approach to business. Accentuating the negative is not without peril. Care must be taken. Needless to say I never exercised any such care, but I would not recommend following my lead. Doing this may be hazardous to your career.

What does it mean to accentuate the negative? It's straightforward. Regardless of your role within an organization, whether it be in product planning or developing tactical responses to market changes, always consider the potential downside of any decision. On the surface this may seem obvious. But as obvious as it may be, it is rarely followed for reasons that will be explained shortly.

Thinking through a problem with an eye toward what can go wrong provides a way to validate and fine tune decisions and strategies. It will also allow you to better estimate the probability of success. In analyzing a plan you may realize there are so many things that could go wrong that it simply won't work. Or, you may find the basic plan is solid if some adjustments are made.

Your analysis should not stop after you identify the things that can go wrong. You also want to weigh the probability of each problem occurring. This will provide a prioritization of the possible occurrences from the most to the least likely. Reviewing both the number of potential problems and their chances of happening will give you a better sense for a plan's overall prospects.

Last but not least, if something does go wrong you'll be prepared. It won't be a surprise. You would have considered the potential impact and hopefully thought about a response strategy in advance.

This approach is somewhat analogous to Andy Grove's concept of needing to be paranoid to survive. For those unfamiliar with Andy Grove, he was one of the founders of Intel Corporation and, as president and CEO, is credited for managing them to a leadership position in the processor business. Intel processors drive the majority of personal computers built today.

In his book, *Only the Paranoid Survive*, Grove talks about his tendency to worry about a range of issues. He worries about products getting messed up or being introduced at the wrong time. He worries about too much production capacity or factories not performing well. He worries about attracting the right people and morale issues. And he worries about competitors. Now that's a whole lot of worrying going on, but you get the concept.

The reason for referencing Mr. Grove is to point out one could easily consider his approach a negative one. Our society considers paranoia a psychological problem. Why would you intentionally go around being paranoid? Well, for good reason. In business, there are always companies trying to steal market share. That is the objective of the game. Everyone wants to increase his or her piece of the pie.

Despite this basic tenant of business, more often than you think, companies who attain a leadership position tend to become complacent. They start believing their own press and think no one can knock them from their perch. If you come across a company with that mentality, steer clear. It's only a matter of time before somebody does knock them off. The key to sustaining success is ensuring you never lose the edge or hunger that got you there in the first place.

My point is similar. Be prepared for things to go wrong because, as Murphy so eloquently put it, *whatever can go wrong, will*. Think about it. The worst thing that can happen is everything actually goes as planned and you never have to react to potential problems or initiate contingency measures. We should all be so lucky.

An example everyone can relate to illustrates the value of this approach. Pilots spend a great deal of time in flight simulators honing their skills. I don't claim any expertise in aviation but I suspect a good portion of that time is spent practicing emergency situations – an engine burns out, the hydraulic system malfunctions, wind shear. These are all potential negative occurrences. No one wants to think about them, but answer this question, *would you rather fly with a pilot who constantly worries about what can go wrong and is prepared to deal with the possibilities, or would you rather fly with a pilot who thinks the world is wonderful and nothing is ever going to go wrong?*

Without conducting any scientific polling, I think it's safe to say the vast majority of people want a pilot prepared for an emergency. Why would it be different in the business world? Particularly in marketing where the objective is to develop products and strategies aimed at penetrating new markets or enhancing existing ones. To do that, you need to be fully prepared. The best laid plans will invariably need to be modified. No one can anticipate every occurrence.

Markets continually evolve and a myriad of factors can shift at any time. A competitive company can unexpectedly announce a new product. Companies may alter their pricing and distribution strategies. Economic conditions can change, affecting buying patterns. A company can even come out of left field with a better mousetrap. The bottom line is the chances are extremely high you will need to react to some event. What better way to do that than to have thought about the possibilities in advance?

I'm not suggesting you devote months in an effort to think of every possible occurrence. This is not only impossible but also would be a colossal waste of time. If something has a one percent chance of occurring don't spend much time thinking about it. I simply suggest early in the planning process time be devoted to examining those things most likely to go wrong, along with their respective probabilities of occurrence.

This sounds intuitive so why waste time talking about it? It's basic, but most people don't think much about the downside. There are several reasons for this; however there is only one valid reason. The valid concern is that going through this *what if* analysis can slow down the planning process. This may be true, but the investment in time will pay significant dividends down the road. It may even save as much or more time at the back end.

It is important to balance the need to conduct an adequate analysis within the context of the time constraints. Done correctly, the analytical process should not substantially delay things. Much of it can be done in parallel with other efforts.

What are the other reasons this analysis isn't done, the ones that are completely bogus? One of them is it takes effort. It is not the path of least resistance. This should never be a deterrent, but people always look for shortcuts. This is an easy shortcut to take since there is no immediate gratification to be gained. All the upside is down the road so *screw it*.

Reinforcing this slothful attitude is the last, and possibly primary reason: people (i.e. management) just don't want to hear about what can go wrong. There is a tendency to reward happy thoughts. Discussing potential problems can create a negative perception. It can fracture the illusion management likes to maintain that everything is wonderful and will ultimately work out. They love *can do* people who provide positive reinforcement for every decision, large and small. The only problem with maintaining this mutual admiration, the world is our oyster mentality, is it will only be a matter of time before something does go wrong. And guess what? None of these delusional thinkers will be prepared to act.

Anyone who has spent any time working in a corporate environment has heard the terms *crisis management* and *fighting fires*. In many companies this is a way of life. Employees go from one fire to the next. It can become a corporate culture.

At times it's unavoidable, you will have to deal with crises. The objective is to minimize the number of them. Operating in crisis mode is inefficient and eventually leads to higher stress levels and lower productivity. By spending a bit more time up front, playing devils advocate, you can avoid crisis management as a way of life. It's that simple.

But the corporate game is to tell management what they want to hear. And it's only natural to want to hear good news. The consequence is management either doesn't know what's going on or worse yet, they develop a false sense of security thinking everything's fine.

Logically, one would think a primary responsibility of management is to manage. This includes being aware of the current status and asking the tough questions. Logic may dictate that but reality does not. Don't take my word for it. Let me reference a respected business expert's own words. In reading these words think of what your confidence level would be in someone who would take such a position.

To avoid any copyright infringement issues I am paraphrasing; however the location of the exact reference is provided at the end of this chapter. Here is the gist of what this individual had to say:

> It can be compared to sailing and the winds change. But you don't notice the wind has changed. Maybe

this is because you're below deck. And because you're below deck you don't feel the wind shift until the boat starts tipping over.

This expert goes on to say something like this:

> Middle management, particularly sales managers who routinely deal with people and situations outside the company, are frequently the first to figure out what worked in the past isn't working anymore. These middle managers often have difficulty expressing their thoughts to senior management. For this reason, senior management is sometimes late in understanding things have changed. And it's not unusual for the CEO to be the last to know.

Who is responsible for these enlightened business concepts? Well none other than the chairman of Intel, Andy Grove himself. How's that for a kick in the pants. One of most respected businessmen in the world, and one who is now responsible for teaching our very finest youth at Stanford University, talking about being below deck when his boat is about to capsize. Hey Andy, why weren't you worried about the wind?

When I read this I could not believe my eyes. My first reaction was what the hell are you doing down below! Who is steering the ship! The answer to that question is nobody and that conclusion was further reinforced by the incredible admission that the CEO is the last to know. I have to give Mr. Grove credit for being brave enough to admit it because, unfortunately, it is true.

Let's give Mr. Grove the benefit of the doubt and assume he was referring to CEOs other than himself when discussing the fact that they don't know what's going on in the company, no less in their market. How do you explain the sail boat example? How does someone in his position use such an absurd example to explain why his company failed to recognize the *change of seas* that had occurred?

A ship's captain is solely responsible for his or her boat just as a CEO is solely responsible for his or her company. There should be no excuses, particularly ignorance. Being down below when your ship is in motion is a dereliction of duty. Sure, even a captain needs to sleep, but when they wake up shouldn't they ask the second in command for a status report? Or, in the case of an emergency, shouldn't the captain be notified immediately?

Hasn't Mr. Grove ever watched an episode of *Star Trek*? The first officer whether it was Mr. Spock or Number 1 always told the captain what was going on. Maybe that's why the Enterprise never got blown up.

Could it be the captain is down below because he/she doesn't want to know what's going on? Can you say plausible deniability? Is it that management is looking for a built in excuse to deflect blame when things go wrong? You know, the "I wasn't informed", or "my subordinates failed to brief me" routine.

You know what? That's a load of crap. It is management's duty to know what's going on.

Management has two primary responsibilities. One is to develop a strategy and set a direction for the company. The second is to manage the execution of that strategy. A "don't ask don't tell" policy may be fine for the military but it has absolutely no place in business.

Mr. Grove also fails to enlighten us as to why middle management finds it hard to explain things to senior management. I'll take a stab at that. Could it be senior management doesn't want to hear it and has a tendency to react negatively to potentially bad news?

This is especially true when a company is experiencing good times. When a company is doing well, management is generally not receptive to any suggestions of potential problems. Problems, what problems? Did you see our last quarterly report! We're freaking geniuses! Didn't anybody tell you! The possibility of having to alter current business conduct to avoid future negative consequences simply doesn't resonate.

I'm not suggesting management be involved in the minutia of business. That is not their role. Neither am I suggesting the people responsible for doing the work should bother management with every little problem or issue. But management at all levels is responsible for understanding what is going on in their respective areas.

Theoretically, information should be passed up the management chain. Eventually it should reach the senior staff, who are then obligated to inform the president/CEO. Granted, the CEO may be the last to know but the delay should not be significant. And I submit if the CEO is truly doing the job he or she should not be the last to know because they should be challenging the staff to make sure everyone is staying on top of their respective areas. Not knowing is tantamount to incompetence in my book and any senior manager who falls back on a lack of awareness as an excuse should be summarily fired.

I'm not advocating adopting a "sky is falling" attitude or preaching gloom and doom. There is a difference between thoroughly understanding all the actions and reactions of a decision and being pessimistic. There is absolutely no place for pessimism. If you don't believe in the ability to ultimately succeed, get out. You have no business in business. The problem is there seems to be a general inability to discern the difference between pessimism and preparation.

My position is everyone, including management, needs to constantly assess the state of the company and industry. At all levels people should be asking the tough questions and demanding answers. Only by doing so can an organization be truly prepared and avoid operating in crisis mode. And my suggestion to Mr. Grove: You might want to go up top and see what's really going on.

A FOOTNOTE TO THIS CHAPTER:

It's funny. I wasn't planning to read Mr. Grove's book but a friend of mine suggested, and correctly so, that if I was going to reference it I should read it. I was faced with either removing the reference or reading the book. In an ironic twist of fate reading his book brought my level of confidence to new heights. It provided a wealth of new material and so perfectly illustrated many of the concepts espoused in my own book.

It was like manna from heaven. I now had documented evidence to support my basic theories of business.

To top it off, it came from a person considered one of the elite in corporate management – a person teaching a graduate course in business at Stanford no less. No wonder those kids graduate and don't know their ass from their elbow when it comes to the realities of business. They're all down below hoping someone else will keep the boat from sinking! Thank you god and Mr. Grove.

I apologize to Mr. Grove about my less than flattering reference to his book and extend an offer to discuss my views with him any time, any place. I am a cocky, err, confident bastard.

FYI. The exact references can be found in *Only The Paranoid Survive*, First Currency Paperback Edition: April 1999. The sailboat reference is on page 20 toward the bottom. The reference to maagement's general ignorance is on page 21 at very the bottom.

CHAPTER TWELVE

Who Do You Work For?

The question of who you work for should not be terribly controversial. Everyone has a boss. Your boss has a boss. The chain of command leads up to the president/CEO and ultimately to the board of directors. So it's clear right? The CEO sets a course for the company. He or she in turn instructs the staff, and eventually it gets to you through your superior. If management tells you to do something you do it.

I guess that's one of the many areas in which I went astray. Here is a point of view you won't hear expressed much at the water cooler. The traditional corporate chain of command philosophy reminds me a little of Nazi Germany. You know, the old "I was only following orders" routine. Now, I in no way want to equate the business world with the atrocities of the Nazi regime. It's just the best example I could think of for the point I want to make.

It's not a point that's going to win me, or you, any friends. Or help either of our respective careers. Right up front, again, I don't recommend you follow in my footsteps. All I hope to accomplish is to provoke some thought and point out that at times it might not only be appropriate, but your responsibility to question management's decisions.

I never felt I worked for the management team. They don't own the company. They are hired just like every other employee (with the exception of company founders). They serve at the discretion of the stockholders. Remember them? Stockholders, the people who actually own the company. For some strange reason I always felt I worked for the stockholders. My responsibility was to perform in a fashion that would benefit them and not necessarily the management team.

Sure, the stockholders theoretically hire the board of directors who in turn hire the management team and so on and so forth. It's not unlike electing a political representative – with one exception: most stockholders don't really have a clue what goes on. Very few ever attend a stockholder's meeting. Many if not most never vote or just tender their proxy.

The end result is a lack of accountability to the stockholders. Boards of directors, whose sole responsibility is to protect the shareholders, rarely spend more than one or two days each quarter thinking about the company they represent. Sure, some board members are major stockholders; however many outside board seats have become perks for well-connected people or people who can bring cachet to the organization.

Even if you believe most boards are genuinely conscientious about protecting the stockholders, the unfortunate truth is the board often doesn't know what the real problems are. The information they get is *filtered* by the management team. If a company is having problems or is under performing do you think the management team is ever going to tell the board they are the problem? Or is it more likely they will find other reasons (or scapegoats) for the company's woes?

Generally, the management team spins the information provided to the board to reflect most positively on its ability to manage the company. In good times or bad, management will undoubtedly have excuses and answers to offer the board. And since the whole board of directors environment is one of consensus, unless you have everyone in agreement, nothing gets changed. It's really a case of the fox watching the chicken coop. You take care of me and I'll take care of you and to hell with the average stockholder.

I don't pretend to be the defender of the little guy. You

won't find me waving the flag for many causes. So don't get the idea that I'm some sort of altruistic guy. Far from it. But when I take a job I take the responsibility very seriously. I have believed and will always believe that my responsibility is to the stockholder and lies in doing everything possible to maximize the return for the stockholder, with an emphasis on the long term.

I have never viewed the direction I received from my boss or my boss' boss or even the freaking CEO as something I should blindly implement, and so, as you might expect, I've never blindly followed orders. I have questioned many of the management teams I've been associated with. I've challenged them to do the right thing. I've identified problems and offered solutions regardless of how politically damaging my actions may have been. And when I believed the management team has had their collective heads up their collective asses, I've told them so. Most of the time, more diplomatically, but not always.

Why? Certainly not because I would personally benefit. Quite the contrary. Invariably, these have been *kamikaze* missions. This attitude makes me a maverick, and mavericks are not embraced in the corporate world. They are considered a destabilizing influence and detrimental to those whose primary goal is to maintain control.

Now you might question such behavior. You could easily argue that being a maverick is not a positive thing. It does create friction and a certain amount of order is necessary for companies to function. All of that is true. And if I were a maverick simply because I had to have things my way or because all I cared about was myself I would agree with you. But that has never been the case. I challenged management because I felt responsible to my true boss, the stockholders. Now you know why I consult.

Food for thought.

CHAPTER THIRTEEN

A Man's Got To Know His Limitations: The Demise of the XFL

When the announcement came that a new football league was forming I greeted it with the usual reaction of a football fan: here we go again.

I mean it's not like it hasn't been tried before. Only once has it been successful and that was in a very different time. The AFL successfully challenged the NFL and ultimately forced a merger thanks in large part to the brashness and talent of Joe Willie Namath and the '69 New York Jets. The USFL also had some modest success lasting three seasons in the 1980s before folding. But that was then and this is now. The NFL is as powerful as it has ever been. Challenging it could only lead to failure. Or maybe not.

There was something different about this new league. First, the king of wrestling, Vince McMahon, was the creator and NBC was a co-investor. NBC's involvement ensured much-needed TV exposure and Mr. McMahon has proven he knows how to put on a show. He had transformed the Worldwide Wrestling Federation (WWF) from a niche pseudo *sporting event* into a mega sports entertainment extravaganza with an enormous following of prime demographics. You may not care for the shtick. I'm right with you. I don't have any use for wrestling. Still, from a purely business standpoint, you have to admire it as a huge turnaround story.

Logically, with a promoter like McMahon and NBC to televise it, the league had at least a chance to take hold. A key aspect was they weren't trying to compete directly against the

NFL as previous leagues had done. The XFL season was scheduled during a general lull in major sporting events. The games started right after the NFL season finale Super Bowl and ended in late April just prior to the beginning of the baseball season. This made a great deal of sense because it positioned the XFL not as a direct competitor to the NFL but as a complement to other sporting events.

This is a business tactic that can work in many situations. If you're faced with a powerful and well-entrenched competitor, it may not be viable to go head-to-head; however that does not mean there is no opportunity to make money with a similar product. What the XFL did was position itself to go around the NFL by targeting a *hole* in their strategy as it were. Sometimes you can make a viable business from the crumbs the big boys leave behind. It may not be glamorous but it can be profitable. The point is, don't assume there is no way to profit. Be creative and look for alternative approaches.

More important than the XFL's strategy to avoid a head-on collision with the NFL was the fact they already had an audience to leverage. And not just any audience, the goldmine of all audiences: males aged 18-34 and teenagers aged 12-17. Nothing is more valuable to a new business enterprise than having an existing customer base to leverage.

All the elements were there for the XFL to be successful. They had guaranteed TV coverage, they had sufficient capital, they had identified an untapped market window, and they had an audience just waiting for the games to begin. The only thing left was to figure out exactly what form the product would take.

First and foremost, unlike wrestling matches where the outcome is preordained, the games would be legit. This was *guaranteed* by the fact Vegas planned to have betting lines on the game. The professional gambling industry would not have touched the XFL with the proverbial 10-foot pole if there were any hint of a fix.

The promotions leading to the premiere promised a different brand of football. There would be no pansy-ass fair catches. The players would be playing for the love of the game, not just going through the motions to collect a seven-figure paycheck. And of course, there would be hot babes, *er* cheerleaders, to root the home team on. All the necessary elements were there: violence and sex. A one-two punch in a society where, alas, only one is necessary to achieve financial success.

For good measure, the league featured some legitimate innovations. The XFL broke new ground with interesting camera angles and they promised fans a glimpse of what it's like to be in the locker room at half time. Given all this, I, for one, thought the league had a chance to be financially successful. I didn't believe for one minute they posed any threat to the NFL, but I thought they could put on a good enough show to make money.

Opening day came and like many fans, curiosity prompted me to watch. Ratings for the initial game were good. The league was off to a promising start…for about 15 minutes, which is all I, and many others, could stand to watch of a very bad product. Now, I didn't expect high-quality football, but I did expect some entertaining moments. I expected a show with a little football thrown in. It didn't happen. What I got was bad football televised with unique camera angles.

Oh there were token attempts to liven up the show. The players, in lieu of their names, were permitted to put anything they wanted on the back of their jerseys. There was no lack of creativity. How can anyone who saw that first game forget *He Hate Me*? Yes, that's right, He Hate Me. At the time I couldn't even tell you the player's name or anything about him. All I remembered was his jersey. Later in the research process I discovered the gentleman's name was Rod Smart, and he did manage to have his 15 minutes and give the league something to focus on, but it was short lived.

One problem was when Mr. Smart was interviewed about his selection of the phrase He Hate Me. He unfortunately could not live up to his name and some very unintelligible drivel came out. You see, most of the players were not Phi Beta Kappa. Hell, they weren't even Phi. These were ex-jocks who weren't good enough to make it in the big leagues. And here's some news, they were not exactly cream of the crop intellectually either. Most of them were probably driving trucks or doing odd jobs before the XFL. No disrespect to truck drivers. It's an honest profession with significant value to society. The point is how many truck drivers would you be interested in hearing interviewed on national TV? Unless they just jumped an 18-wheeler over the Grand Canyon, probably zero.

But that wasn't the primary reason the league failed so miserably after only one season. The league was brain dead after opening day. Ratings fell like a rock. Even a mid-season attempt to liven things up by sneaking a glimpse into the cheerleaders' locker room at half time wasn't enough to resuscitate interest. This was mostly because, as I understand it, there was nothing to see. Yet another disappointment for the testosterone-laden 12 to 34-year-old males who comprised the primary target market.

What went wrong? A very basic thing. The league didn't leverage its strength – its installed base. The XFL had a huge audience of prime demographics just waiting for a follow-on product to their beloved wrestling. All it had to do was duplicate the WWF formula to keep that audience.

The XFL did not do that, not by a long shot. It wasn't a

violent spectacle and there wasn't nearly enough sex. It was just boring football. I'm guessing here, but I suspect McMahon got it in his head he could actually show the NFL a thing or two. Ego may have played a part. Regardless, he lost sight of his strengths and that was the fatal mistake. He didn't know his limitations. McMahon isn't a football man. He isn't even a sports guy. His strength is being a *showman*. He should have leveraged that talent and leveraged his existing base.

Regardless of the industry or product, these are two very important points applicable to a broad range of business situations. *You need to understand your personal strengths and weaknesses.* You also need to understand the strengths and weaknesses of your company. The best way to increase your chance of success is to play to your strengths and compensate for your weaknesses. In the case of one's personal strengths, the goal is to seek ways to leverage what you're good at and avoid doing things you're not very good at.

In Mr. McMahon's case he had proven to be very good at putting on a show. He had no experience and evidently no particular skills in putting on a sporting event. Yet he seemed to get caught in the middle and failed to do what he did best. Mr. McMahon is by no means alone in making this mistake. It's quite common. Everyone needs to understand what their strengths and weaknesses are so they can put themselves in a position to best apply their strengths and avoid or improve their areas of weakness.

This is particularly true for people in management. A good manager should always try to augment their skills by ensuring there are team members with complementary skills. It is important for the entire team to have a balanced set of skills. The last thing you want to have is a team where everyone has the same strengths and weaknesses. This creates holes in the team's ability and will undoubtedly lead to problems.

The other point relates to companies and products. *When you have existing products and customers, the first opportunity you should explore is developing new products to fit your existing base.* This is the easiest way to increase a company's revenue. By doing this you won't have to alter your sales or marketing strategies and you won't have to spend any money on identifying and communicating to new customers. Always look for products that fit your base first.

The XFL had a prime opportunity to bring another entertainment-oriented product to their customer base. Instead, they attempted to create a *legitimate* sports product. It was the proverbial square peg in a round hole. It was totally avoidable.

The XFL didn't need to go so far as to fix the games like they do with wrestling matches. By the same token, they couldn't take the football too seriously either. How could they? All you need to do is apply some common sense.

Football is like any other product. Here, the product is the team and the level of play of the athletes. What attracts most fans is watching people who are the best in the world at what they do. You can argue what they do isn't important or even very interesting. Nonetheless, they are the best in the world. For a true sports fan, watching the best compete at anything is interesting.

The XFL could never have hoped to put the highest quality on the field. All the best players already had high-paying jobs. The XFL was paying chump change. The only way for the players to make any money was to win the championship game. No quality athlete would be attracted under those circumstances.

And before anyone gets on a high horse about me being derogatory toward the XFL players, in fairness to them, they were fine athletes. Many of them were probably quality high school or college players. They tried as hard as they could to perform at a high level.

Let's face it, most of them were probably hoping for a shot at playing for the NFL. The XFL was, if nothing more, an opportunity for them to showcase their talent. A handful of players did manage to get NFL jobs. But they could never hope to play up to NFL standards as a team; therefore to a sports fan, it would not be very interesting if they played it straight.

Given the XFL could not produce a quality product, they had to find another way to leverage their audience. They didn't have to search very far. All they had to do was to duplicate what was working all along.

Put on a damn show! Forget about the game *per se*. Create personalities for each team. This would give people a rooting interest despite the level of quality. You know, the old *heroes and villains* routine that has served pro wrestling so well. Seed the teams with enough players and coaches willing and able to articulate that personality. Admittedly, this would require the players and coaches to operate with the understanding their jobs were more to put on a show than to play football. Oh sure, play the game and try to win, but the number one priority should have been the show.

To execute this strategy the league needed to alter the game sufficiently to create a show while still maintaining some semblance of a football game. What could they have done? Well they had a good start with the new camera angles and locker room visits. Unfortunately, they screwed up the locker room visits. Here they had a perfect opportunity to *stage* something interesting for the fans. Instead, they played it straight. What you saw were coaches actually talking to their teams. And just as the players were not of the highest caliber, there were no Bill

Parcells among the coaching ranks. Come on. What were they thinking? Throw a chair, bust up some lockers. Let's see some violence!! Where's the fake blood when you need it?

They also could have done more to make the game interesting. The elimination of the fair catch was a good idea but it wasn't nearly enough. Maybe they could have done some crazy things like force the teams to go no huddle for one quarter.

I guess I should apologize to those of you who don't follow football. But I'm not going to. Go to the next chapter or look it up. It would disrupt my stream of consciousness to explain everything. Besides, I'm not writing a chapter on the XFL just because I'm a sports fan. The XFL was a huge business opportunity lost, and therefore a good case study. The sports aspects are peripheral.

Oh and lest I forget, beef up the sex. I mean the cheerleaders had on way too much clothing, and they didn't get nearly enough airtime. And come up with some entertaining cheers. You get the point.

The bottom line is if the XFL had played to its strength and catered to (dare I say marketed itself to) an audience already predisposed to *buy* the product, they could have been a financial success if not a serious football league. And what was the point in the first place? I thought it was to make money.

CHAPTER FOURTEEN

Consensus Management:
To Serve or Protect?

The term consensus management is widely known and is as widely practiced. But what are its true goals? Consensus management is where a designated group of decision makers assembles to solve a problem or make a decision. The theory is you get everyone to agree on a course of action before proceeding. Sounds great on paper.

Then again so does communism. In fact, consensus management and communism share a few traits. Just as communism takes away all incentive to apply oneself to achieve a better life, consensus management takes away all incentive to be creative, to push the envelope, and to take personal responsibility for decisions and actions. That is, unless you have an entire team of people who think alike. But that tends to be pretty rare.

Hold on a minute. I'm not being fair to consensus management. The objective is to ensure all points of view are considered and everyone feels comfortable with the decision. Getting everyone to *buy in* fosters better teamwork and cohesive execution. That's what you'll read in most business books. But this isn't most business books. This is the business book from the dark side.

Consensus management does sound good in theory. The philosophy is solid. But that forces me to refer, once again, to communism. Philosophically, communism can sound attractive as well. If someone told you they could eliminate poverty and allow everyone to have an acceptable standard of living simply by following a strategy of mutual sharing, cooperation, and participation, doesn't that sound attractive? That's communism in a nutshell. Great concept, but it just doesn't work as an economic system.

And consensus management doesn't work as a management system. Oh, there are some environments where consensus management is viable. A governing body like the United Nations is an example. Being comprised of independent countries, cooperation is only possible if participants know decisions cannot be forced upon them. Thus, the key UN members who comprise the Security Council have veto power. Without it, the organization would likely collapse.

Generally, environments made up of independent entities are appropriate for consensus management. Industry consortiums are an example in the business community. Consortiums are designed to foster cooperation. They are usually intended to further specific industry goals. Their very existence relies on the knowledge that decisions cannot be forced on the members. The net result is an organization that takes a great deal of time to achieve its goals – if it's able to achieve them at all. Many industry consortiums fail. But that's fine. If a consortium fails no one is any worse off than they were before.

The federal government works on a consensus basis. Need I say more? I will anyway. Consensus in the form of compromise is a good idea when applied to the government. It limits the potential damage politicians can do.

I once thought it would be great if one party controlled every aspect of government. Then things could get done. That was before I realized both parties and most politicians couldn't manage their way out of a paper bag. They are so driven by the fringe elements within their parties they become dangerous if allowed control. History has proven this to be the case time and again. So in government, it's good we have a system that forces consensus and compromise. It prolongs action and waters down decisions, minimizing their eventual impact.

But business is not like politics. In business, you don't have the luxury of taking months or years to make decisions and execute strategies. Businesses can't print money or run huge deficits. Survival depends on the ability to react quickly. The decision-making process needs to be streamlined not complicated.

I would agree that consensus management should be an objective for businesses. It just shouldn't ever be mandated. Under some circumstances, it may even work, though I struggle to think of an example that applies. A merger or acquisition decision might be one. Maybe a company should not proceed if the entire senior staff doesn't agree. This type of decision is not specific to any individual department or organization. It affects the whole. So an argument can be made there should be a consensus. But even here I would argue this type of decision is the responsibility of the CEO. The CEO should consider all inputs, then do what he or she feels is best for the company.

Here's another thought I'm sure you'll do back flips over. You know what the most efficient form of leadership is? A dictatorship. That's right. One person makes all the decisions. No necessity to consult. No committees to form. No consensus to achieve. Just one person. Decisions can be made in seconds in a dictatorship.

Oh my god, what is this idiot advocating? We should operate under a dictatorship? No, I merely stated that dictatorships were the most efficient form of leadership. I didn't say they were the best. History has repeatedly proven dictatorships tend to be bad things. I don't personally know of any that have been good. There may have been one, but it would be the exception not the rule.

Dictatorships are not bad because the system is inherently

bad. They are bad because, for whatever reason, the people who seek power tend to be bad. Or, as they say, power corrupts and absolute power corrupts absolutely. That seems to be the case.

Just think how much we could get accomplished if there were such a person as a benevolent dictator. Someone completely focused on improving the world, without personal motivations. A person who understands the way to do that is to assemble a team of talented people and empower them to do what they do best. Oversee, guide, facilitate, and make the tough decisions when necessary, but let the people under them do their jobs. Won't happen in our lifetime. Maybe some day we'll be civilized enough to operate that way.

Anyway back to business. What was I saying before I got on my soapbox about the failings of human nature? Oh, consensus management sucks. It doesn't work often enough to make it worthwhile.

Here's my take on how management should work. Everyone is hired to do a job. The higher you go in an organization the more responsibility and authority you have. In theory, people who achieve management positions, whether they are managers, directors, or vice presidents, have gotten there because they have the requisite experience and talent, and someone believes they can do the job. I say in *theory* because that's bullshit. That's not how it works, at least not often enough. But just for yucks, let's make believe that's how it works.

We'll use marketing as an example. It's a good one because everyone thinks they're a *marketeer*. What is the responsibility of a vice president of marketing? In general, that person is tasked with setting a direction for the company with respect to an overall product or business strategy. A marketing person has to make key decisions about what products to bring to market. They have to decide how to use company resources to maximize revenues and profits.

If I had it my way, there would not be any committee making those decisions. It would be the VP of marketing and that person alone. The only person he or she should have to get approval from is the president or CEO. Nobody else.

That is not to say he or she should not consult others. They should consult a range of people including their own team and all the other departments. It is essential to get people's opinions. Again, it's a matter of perspective. Everyone approaches things from a slightly different one.

No one can know everything. It's important to be inclusive in the decision-making process. The problem is not with allowing people to express opinions or even attempting to build consensus. The ideal scenario is to achieve consensus, but consensus building and consensus management are two very different things.

The problem lies in making the decision. That's where I would draw the line. Gather opinions and include that input in the decision-making process. Understand the potential impact a decision may have on other departments. Make every effort to get everyone in agreement. After that, the decision should lie with the responsible person. THAT'S WHAT THEY ARE BEING PAID FOR! Or at least I think that's what they're paid for.

Unlike politicians who can stay in power because of the biases of the election process, or a dictator who stays in power by controlling the military, a manager, at any level, can be fired. Screw up. Get fired. It's doesn't have to be more complex than that. I don't mean make one mistake and you lose your job. But if a person demonstrates over time they don't possess the skills to perform their role, they should be fired. The point is, every manager should be given the chance to do what they feel is right.

Committees and consensus management are inefficient and counterproductive. What is the point of hiring people who are theoretically experts in their field if you're going to require every important decision to be made by a group of people who don't all possess the required expertise?

Why would you want an engineer commenting on a marketing strategy? Or, how valuable is a sales person's opinion on manufacturing issues? Do marketing people go around telling engineers how to design stuff? Some probably do, but they shouldn't. Why? They are not experts. It's not what they are paid to do. Yet companies will invariably make their senior managers, people from varying backgrounds with very different skills sets, agree before proceeding.

If you find yourself in a company where it seems senior management is unable or unwilling to make decisions, and the reason is an inability to build a consensus, watch out. Bad times may be on the horizon. This process can paralyze a company. Decisions are delayed or compromised to the point they become ineffective. The competition will eventually overtake a company operating in this mode.

You want to know why consensus management is popular? Part of the reason is it limits accountability. As a consequence, it provides a higher level of job security. If a decision made by an entire team turns out to be a bad one, what are you going to do? Fire everybody? No. The typical reaction is to say, *oh well, we made a mistake. Better luck next time.* On the other hand, if a single person makes a bad decision, get the blindfold and ask for a last request. They're dead. It will be pack-of-wolves time.

I submit the real reason for consensus management is to protect senior management, not to serve the company. Most senior managers don't have the balls to make decisions. Nor are they willing to take the risk of having their subordinates make them either. It's CYA (cover your ass), not efficient business.

Have I at least made a bit of sense?

CHAPTER FIFTEEN

A Mirror's Reflection

Many parallels exist between the worlds of sport and business. But there exists at least one significant difference. It pertains to the reward systems. In sports, there is an admirable purity of sorts when it comes to rewarding employees (athletes). By and large, in sports, the only thing a team (i.e., company) cares about is how an athlete performs their job.

The same can't be said for most other businesses. Where else could an employee act with almost complete impunity without the fear of risking their career? Athletes can pretty much do anything as long as they continue to perform. The very best athletes can use drugs, miss practices, spit at umpires, evade taxes, even witness a double homicide and obstruct justice without much concern for losing their jobs. Seemingly, there is only one line an athlete can't cross. That line is hitting their wives or girlfriends.

For an excellent example of the level of tolerance sports franchises exhibit one need look no further than Dennis Rodman. Only in the sports or entertainment world could a person like Rodman succeed. Like many, I got a chuckle out of his act for a while. But when he donned that wedding dress he lost me.

Whether or not you like Dennis Rodman is not the issue. The point is he performed his role on the basketball court better than most. The fact he's more than a little strange is inconsequential. I don't condone his lack of discipline or his propensity for missing and disrupting practices. That is unprofessional behavior and should not be tolerated. Conversely, dying your hair purple and acting like a jerk in your personal life in no way impacts your ability to get the job done. Given this, why should an employer care?

As admirable as this philosophy may be, the sports world's motives are unfortunately not driven by a higher standard of ethics or an altruistic belief in fair play. Far from it. The reward system is motivated by the almighty dollar. And the general lack of moral accountability is disconcerting.

World-class athletes are rare. This is why they command such high salaries. It is also the reason a blind eye is turned to their less than stellar behavior. In sports, the primary business goal is to win. The customers or fans care about little else. In most cases, the revenue and profit streams for sports enterprises are predicated on winning. As a consequence, employers pay little attention to an athlete's personal behavior. Even if that behavior happens to break a law along the way. Hell, don't pay your taxes, go smoke some dope. Just win baby. Nothing's perfect. The end result has merit even if the motives are suspect.

The poster boy for the tolerance of sports is a former pitcher named Steve Howe. This guy was suspended seven times for cocaine use and reinstated every time. Why? Because he could still get batters out. I'm all for giving a person a second chance. Everyone deserves the opportunity to correct a mistake, but seven times? Give me a break. That's absurd and the kind of thing that gives sports and athletes a bad name.

I know of only one example where an athlete's behavior resulted in a termination of their contract. That was when Latrell Sprewell choked his coach. Although rarely invoked, sports franchises often put morals clauses in contracts. This is particularly true for high-profile players. I believe the team, at least in part, leveraged the clause to terminate Sprewell. Not that it substantially impacted Latrell. After missing part of one season he was back in the league and thriving with the New

York Knicks.

I wasn't in favor of the Knicks giving Sprewell a chance. As a fan I can tolerate a lot of things. Choking your boss isn't one of them. There were many times I felt like choking my boss but I managed to refrain. Maybe because I know I would have ended up in jail.

I'm not even saying Latrell wasn't partially provoked. The coach, P.J. Carlesimo, apparently did a good job of creating a climate that might result in abhorrent behavior. Translation: P.J. was reportedly a class-A asshole. Still, you need to maintain a semblance of control and walk away. Latrell, it should be noted, has been a model citizen since coming to the Knicks. At least in this case, forgiving such an egregious act appears to have been warranted.

Motives aside, philosophically, the world of sports has a preferred reward system. Their problem is a lack of integrity when it comes to employee conduct. Too often athletes cross the line of generally accepted moral and professional conduct. Interestingly, the corporate world exhibits a reverse kind of behavior. The two worlds are like that of a reflection in a mirror, where the left side becomes the right and vice versa.

In the corporate world, the reward system is not solely based on performance. The higher you go in the corporate hierarchy, the farther the reward system strays from being performance-based. Worse yet, employees are actually rewarded for what I would consider unprofessional behavior.

It's not the same kind of behavior athletes seem prone to exhibit. In business, drugs and criminal activity are rarely the problem. The behavior I'm referring to is of a political and self-serving nature. In business, you could be doing a fine job and meet all your responsibilities but still not be rewarded. People in power can be petty at times. Too often, if you don't at least acknowledge the political aspects of the environment, your ability to advance is greatly diminished.

Compounding the problem is the fact the focus on politics is magnified the higher you go in the organization. The higher up, the more success is based upon *playing the game* rather than performing your job. This is a sad fact of corporate life. It is sad because performance becomes secondary. Worse yet, the wrong behavior is actually reinforced. Politics should never be a consideration. I take that back. It should be a consideration. People should be fired for political acts that hurt the company.

Are you curious why two profit-motivated entities could have such different approaches? I hope so because I'm going to offer a theory.

In sports the customers pay very close attention to the company. Every move sports teams make is reported daily. The customers are so interested in the comings and goings of their teams (companies) they will take time out of their day to keep informed. Every player and management move is watched closely. Not because the fan is interested in the business aspects, but because every move has a potential impact on winning and losing. Management is under a microscope and success is measured day-to-day in the win-loss columns of the sports pages.

Win and they love you. Don't win and management is out. And winning is largely predicated on how good the players are. Ipso facto, all that matters is getting and keeping the best athletes. This is best accomplished by a total focus on performance and rewarding that performance.

In the corporate world, such scrutiny doesn't exist. Customers, by and large, couldn't care less about the inner workings of companies who supply them products. Stockholders care. But they are neither willing nor able to keep abreast of a company's activities on a daily basis. At best, they can review quarterly reports and analyze revenues and earnings. But success is much more difficult to monitor or gauge. The problem is management can make decisions that enhance the financials in the short-term but damage the company in the long-term. Unless you really do your homework this is difficult if not impossible to detect until it's too late.

This leads to behavior that is not necessarily in the best interest of the corporation. There is a tendency for management to make decisions that look to the outside world like the company is on track while in reality the company's future viability is being hurt. Why would anyone do this intentionally? Because management can personally benefit from stock options and bonuses. To succeed in a company operating in this mode requires a willingness to ignore the best interests of the company. Instead, the focus shifts to what is best for management. This is a political act; therefore to advance, you focus on politics versus performance. No better example can be cited than Enron.

What's the point of all of this? There are only two criteria that should be considered in a reward system: performance and professionalism. Performance is self-explanatory. There are three aspects to professionalism: treat everyone fairly, don't break any laws in the course of doing business, and don't play politics. To me, politics is highly unprofessional behavior. The sports world holds to that philosophy to a much greater degree than the business world.

Yes, if the corporate world were just a bit more like the sports world in this regard it would be nice. People being judged based on their contribution and not because they are politically popular. By the same token, if the sports world had higher moral standards that would be nice too.

Something to strive for.

CHAPTER SIXTEEN

Rules of the Game

Another aspect of business that doesn't parallel sports is the lack of a clearly defined set of rules. Rules are invaluable in sports to define acceptable behavior and the overall objectives. The objectives of business are well understood; however the interpretation of what constitutes acceptable behavior varies widely.

I thought I would take a crack at creating a set of rules for business. The proposed rules are a byproduct of two basic principles. One, *we are all ultimately responsible for our own actions*. Not an overly controversial principle, one would think. That used to be the case. These days our litigious society has become expert at placing blame and responsibility on everyone and everything except the individuals involved.

Our mindset has shifted from accepting responsibility to placing blame. There is no better illustration of this than the inane warning labels on practically every product we buy. Or in the fact that some clumsy person can spill coffee on themselves and be awarded millions of dollars because the company who sold them the coffee didn't tell them exactly how hot it was. This behavior is rampant in the business world as well. Management rarely blame themselves for a company's ills. The blame is, invariably, shifted to people lower in the organization or some external force out of their control.

The second basic principle, simply put, is *treat people fairly*. Try to be objective and don't put your personal well being ahead of another person's rights.

You know the old saying, it's not whether you win or lose but how you play the game? In part it's a good theory. The part "how you play the game" is good. I'm not a fan of the "it's not about winning and losing" part. It is about winning. The motivation to win is extremely important. I wouldn't want to work with anyone who doesn't want to win or accepts defeat easily. However, winning should never take precedent over ethical and honest conduct.

I want to win more than most, but as strong as the desire to win is, it has never exceeded the importance of how winning is accomplished. I am proud to have achieved my success without compromising my convictions and in an ethical and honest fashion. For me, personal integrity comes before wealth and power.

I am by no means a religious man. I will never claim to be driven by the belief in a higher authority. Mostly, competitiveness and the desire to experience the satisfaction that can only come from winning *fair and square* is what drives me. There is absolutely no satisfaction in winning through cheating or unfair tactics. This is true in sports and in business. I would never think of cheating at a game to win nor would I *cheat* at business to achieve my career goals. Any victory based on such actions would be completely hollow.

Given this, I offer the following basic rules, sort of The Ten Commandments of Business Conduct, according to Tony:

1. Never take credit for things you haven't done and always give credit to those who deserve it.
2. Never put your own well being above that of the stockholders/owners.
3. Never intentionally harm someone's career for your own benefit.
4. When you make a commitment, do everything you can to make good.

5. Don't abuse a position of authority and power. This applies to individuals in a company and companies within an industry.
6. Don't say something you don't believe just because it's what someone wants to hear.
7. Always try to negotiate deals that are fair to all parties even if you don't have to.
8. Don't intentionally lie to gain an advantage over a competitor.
9. Maintain a separation between business and personal issues. (Personal feelings should never be injected into the decision-making process nor should anyone take what happens in a business environment personally.)
10. If following any of these rules is not in your personal best interest, quit and find another job.

They sound simple and are mostly based on a sense of fair play and honesty. You'd like to think most people could or would abide by these rules, but in business it is not that straight-forward.

At the lower levels of an organization, survival often means taking crap. People at the bottom don't have much choice. They are at the mercy of management. Maintaining a paycheck can often hinge on ensuring their superiors are happy regardless of the abuse endured.

I always make it a point to treat people below me with respect. Their jobs are hard enough without being abused by people with power over them. So rule number 6 is not easy to follow unless you rise high enough in an organization to limit the potential for abuse. Of course, becoming the top dog can eliminate this problem, but that's not a practical solution for most people. The best solution is for management to treat the people below them fairly.

Barring management *seeing the light*, the best recourse to minimize abuse is to move higher up in the pecking order. Oh but here's the rub, the easiest way to do that is to break rules 1, 2, 3, and 6. That may mean breaking one or all of them. It depends on the circumstances and the level of ambition.

I wouldn't say everyone who gets ahead is guilty of this behavior. Mother Teresa managed to make a name for herself without stepping on people. Of course, she didn't exactly hit the jackpot when it came to personal wealth. Unless you count all the good she did for others as personal wealth. Now I'm no Mother Teresa, (I know, you're shocked by that) and I don't know many people in business who are. It is my humble opinion most people break at least one of these rules to accomplish their own objectives. Particularly rule 6. Too often the best way to win favor with the boss is to tell them what they want to hear.

It's also not unusual for rules 7 and 8 to be breached to further a career to the detriment of the company. I have seen a lot of contracts signed that were bad deals. This stems from the reward system for people who are responsible for negotiating contracts. It is not always geared toward signing a good deal but rather to just signing any deal. And who is going to lose any sleep over lying about a competitor to gain an advantage? Some companies make this a way of life.

It's funny, the only time you get a completely accurate gauge of a company's ethics is when you compete against them. When you are not competing or when you partner with a company, everyone tends to be on their best behavior; however when you get into a competitive situation, a company's true colors surface.

You may have sensed I don't have the most favorable opinion of Microsoft and Intel. This has nothing to do with their success. It has everything to do with their conduct. I can tell you from firsthand experience they don't think much of rules 5, 7, and 8.

With today's corporate and political mindset, it is, sadly, much easier to succeed if you don't let completely ethical conduct get in the way. It's human nature to take shortcuts, and these are the kinds of shortcuts that can get you to the top. If all you care about is making big bucks, it's not that hard. Often all it takes is a willingness to *bend the rules* and kiss a little ass along the way. That means your boss, your boss' boss, and everyone up the line you can get within kissing distance of.

You may think these rules are intended to outline a moral code of conduct. They are not. They may focus on conduct but their intent is to create a more efficient and productive business environment.

Ponder this: Suppose there was a mythical company who abided by these rules. Ask yourself a few key questions. Do you think the confidence in being rewarded for their effort would motivate people to work harder? Do you think people would be more efficient because time wouldn't be wasted on issues not focused on the company's goals? Do you think people, in general, would be happier and therefore more productive because they are treated fairly? Do you think the company would benefit from all of this? In my view, the answer to all these questions is yes.

CHAPTER SEVENTEEN

The Moral of the Story

A s highlighted in the introduction, perspective will play a critical role in determining what any individual takes from these pages. My goal was to comment on business at multiple levels. It is impossible to predict which of these levels might resonate with a given reader. I sought to go beyond what is taught in academia or espoused by those at the very top of the corporate hierarchy. In my opinion these perspectives offer the average reader little in the way of practical knowledge. The vast majority of us will never be CEOs. It might be interesting to imagine rising to the top, but there is not a book or course on the planet that will play a significant role in helping anyone actually achieve such a goal.

Much of what can be learned in the classroom and from traditional business books is focused on the mechanical aspects of business. These sources provide instruction in the various disciplines comprising business. We can learn the theoretical pros and cons of various organizational structures and management philosophies. And although this knowledge provides the underpinnings required to function in corporate life, it falls well short of providing the full range of tools necessary to truly understand and deal with the realities that exist in business.

Despite all the years spent in an academic environment, only one course stands out. It was a course entitled organizational behavior, and dealt with the cultural aspects of business. It was a fascinating course because it was the first time anyone had ever raised the specter of the cultural and political component of business, but even that only dealt with the tip of the iceberg.

I hope this book contributes to exposing the rest of that iceberg.

I used the metaphor of the heart, mind, and soul to convey the key influences of business. This metaphor is more appropriate than you may think because organizations are, in a sense, living entities. They gestate, are born, grow, and evolve. Along the way they develop personalities and a sense of ethics. And like humans, they are a product of both social influences and *inherited* traits.

For example, the organizational structure, products, and markets chosen at the outset of an organization's life can be considered inherited traits. Examples of social influences could include external market and economic forces. So viewing an organization as if it were a living entity is quite appropriate.

That being the case, focusing on both the *physical* and *spiritual* components of business is essential to gaining a complete understanding. In our examination of the *soul of business* we touched upon some of the intangibles that have the greatest impact. These related to political and personal motivations, the influences of greed and power, and the somewhat arbitrary nature of what we define as success and celebrity. I even took a stab at estimating the very tangible costs associated with these intangible influences.

The discussion of the *heart* focused on the more mechanical nature of life and business. Given the heart is little more than a living pump, also an appropriate analogy.

I offered a rationale for adopting a marketing-driven philosophy. Some of the key functional aspects of marketing were discussed. Aspects such as product management and product marketing and the skills necessary to perform these functions at a high level were outlined. I also reviewed some of the important global aspects of marketing including branding, public relations, bringing new products to market, and better understanding the role of the Internet.

Lastly, in examining the *mind of business* we probed both the tangible and intangible influences on management. Illustrated were the role of ego, the need to understand both individual and departmental strengths and weaknesses, and the propensity to ignore the downside. I questioned the role and responsibilities of management as well as those being managed. I even offered a possible set of rules that would serve to govern management philosophies and overall corporate conduct.

At the most basic level, throughout the book are practical examples of management and marketing techniques developed from years of hands-on experience. Regardless whether you agree with my philosophical views, it is my hope these will be useful to anyone working in a corporate environment. Undoubtedly, for some, this may be the only aspect found to be useful. I hope that is not the case for most readers.

One level up from the base, the nature of our responsibilities as managers and employees was discussed. It was suggested taking individual responsibility versus seeking the protection of a group was a more appropriate way to meet corporate obligations. An alternative to the traditional way of thinking about our allegiances was proposed with the hope both managers and those being managed might understand it is the stockholder/owner who truly deserves our loyalty.

And, at the highest level, there was an effort to provoke thought on an alternative approach to business. One that fosters the notion that long-term thinking is the true formula for achieving sustainable success. An approach that believes ultimately everyone will benefit more if the good of the organization was put before the personal good. And that using the power of management in a fair and ethical fashion and rewarding individuals for the right reasons just might result in a greater good for all. Not only for individuals, but companies, the economy, and ultimately society as a whole.

What you, as a reader, take from these concepts will depend on your belief system and career aspirations. I would not presume to tell you how to conduct yourself. I can only offer my conduct and the lessons learned as an example. If you take away nothing else, I hope this book has served to increase the sense of awareness and understanding of how the intangibles of corporate culture, human emotion, and personal motivations impact the business environment.

The superiority of capitalism as an economic system is unquestionable. The economic machine resulting from the systemic design of our corporate environment is second to none. But like all aspects of life, there is always room for improvement. Doing so will take us to greater heights and solidify our leadership position in the world. And if this book acts as a catalyst to at least create a dialog about altering our overall mindset and behavior, then it will have achieved its ultimate goal.

What's at the Bottom of that Cracker Jack Box?

When I started writing this book I didn't have a plan. I was doing nothing more than recording my experiences hoping they would be interesting enough to warrant attention.

Not having a solid product plan was certainly a problem. Without it, all that existed were the basic elements to create a product. There was no distinct target market or clear product positioning. This is tantamount to a company developing a product just because it can. Not because the product fills a need. Clearly, that is not a formula for success. Fortunately, ideas materialized and the book evolved into a real product.

This was, in large part, due to the invaluable feedback received throughout the process from friends and colleagues. As with any good product development process, this one was an evolving effort. Feedback was garnered and adjustments were made. As time went on, the audience of reviewers grew, and a broader range of demographics was represented.

Gathering the feedback was only half the equation. The other half was in evaluating the data. This required objectivity. If emotion crept in, the chance for success would diminish. This is true for any product development. It's common for people to get too close to the product. They begin viewing it as their *baby* and start personalizing things.

In the case of this book that problem was magnified. This *was* personal. It was not easy to be objective. Many of the reviewers were friends. One was even an ex-girlfriend – probably not the best idea but I needed the perspective of a sensitive person. The *touchy feely* demographic as it were, since it is blatantly obvious that is an area in which I possess no expertise.

Under any circumstances you can't be completely objective. We all have biases, and some are going to filter through. But with a little effort you can strip away most biases, and doing so is critical to consistently making good decisions. Subjectivity is never the preferred choice. More often than not, subjectivity allows error to creep in to the decision-making process.

The good news was much of the feedback was positive, making it far easier to be objective. As ideas emerged, I used this group of reviewers as a sounding board from which to solicit various perspectives. I never *assumed* any of my ideas were good. I was too close to the product. Other opinions were necessary to validate every idea. A positive response to integrating sports and other ideas dictated their inclusion.

By following this process, the product concept took shape and key elements finally existed to enhance the overall value. Coupled with the *edgy* style, the book took on a unique slant. I should note, I didn't conscientiously set out to create that edge. It came naturally. Fortunately, in this case I thought my *attitude* might actually be a positive.

Initial shortcomings aside, I did possess at least one key element important to success. I was leveraging my strengths. The book combined two personal passions, marketing and sports, subjects I knew well. This is critical in bringing any product to market. It was the main point raised in the chapter about the XFL. The goal should always be to identify company and individual strengths and target products and markets that best utilize those strengths.

Conversely, companies should not normally go after opportunities where they have no particular strengths. No matter how large they may be. If a company feels they cannot ignore a potential opportunity in an area in which they possess no core competencies, then they should acquire those competencies before embarking on such an endeavor.

Then, the final key element surfaced: confidence. I asked myself, *why doubt your abilities now*? I've never thought I was going to fail before. Not to say I've never failed. I have. Everybody has. What's the old saying, if you've never failed you've never tried. If you never extend yourself or take a risk you can do an adequate job of avoiding failure. The key to success is not avoiding failure. It is minimizing your failures, learning from them, and proceeding to challenge yourself again. So why should this challenge end in failure, particularly since I was writing about what I do best? I just had to stop thinking like a neophyte author and start thinking like someone creating a product.

Despite the objective probability of it all, I began to think it could work. This was in large part due to two interesting aspects that had evolved. Little *surprises* not unlike finding the prize at the bottom of a Cracker Jack box.

The first was the combination of sports and business. On the surface you might think this was nothing more than a byproduct of my personal interests. You know, typical male behavior injecting itself into the writing process.

Ah, but a closer look reveals including sports made perfect sense and was integral to understanding the *soul of business*. Beyond the parallels and analogies, sports and business are, in essence, the same thing. The objectives are identical; both are about competing and winning. The only difference is, in business it is not by physical means but by intellectual ones.

For me, business has never been work *per se*. It has been a playing field. I never excelled at athletics. I don't possess size, strength or speed. And no, I can't jump. Sport was never going to put a roof over my head. Heck, it wouldn't even buy a night at a Motel 6.

Fortunately the business world provided an arena to fuel my competitive fires. Just as in sport, business is a team of people trying to beat another team of people. The scorecard is profit and loss and market share.

Those who treat business in the same fashion as sport and compete with the same passion as athletes, have an advantage over those who view it as just a job. The competitiveness, the aggressiveness, the killer instinct, these are the things that separate the *men from the boys*. So integrating sports into the book wasn't tangential. It was a key component of one of the central points.

There was another, even more interesting surprise. This one pertained to one of the book's subjects. A subject that ultimately served a dual purpose. What is this book about? Is this book about a marketer's perspective or is it merely an exercise in marketing a book? Did I set out to provide useful information or did I use my expertise to create a self-contained lesson in marketing? What if I told you the book by itself is nothing more than a microcosm of the business process and is a stand-alone lesson in marketing or *the heart of business*?

A brief review of some of the content reveals that clues were sprinkled throughout:

- In the introduction, the book's product definition was described.
- The reasons for selecting the subject for the first chapter were included in the chapter, and they were twofold. First, the subject was selected to quickly engage the reader. This is a primary goal of many products. The second was it represented the main theme of the book. Given this, it was

a logical choice to start the book. These were specific product decisions designed to enhance the overall product value.

- The logic and thought process behind incorporating "commercials" along with their intended goals were discussed. This is also a key product decision. It touched upon the promotional and positioning aspects of the product. The concept of a unique selling proposition was introduced, as was the importance of a unique feature set. This represents a real-world example of the types of decisions made every day in the course of defining and bringing a product to market.

- The decision to reposition the book to include sports as a secondary theme was openly discussed. This discussion included the reasons behind the decision and the potential impact on the target market. This is nothing more than an illustration of the process of identifying a specific target market and ensuring the product's positioning is consistent with that market.

- Finally, in the beginning of this epilogue, we summarized the product development process. It was noted the book (or product) constantly evolved based on feedback and changing market conditions. This exemplifies a typical development process and reinforces the critical point of leveraging core competencies.

These insights into the product development process serve to demonstrate the procedures businesses throughout the world follow to define, position, and sell a product. The subject and the product are interwoven. Thus, the book itself can be viewed as a practical example of the complete product/marketing cycle.

Assuming you bought this book, didn't we succeed in demonstrating how to, in fact, market a product? If success in marketing is manifested by the sale of a product then the purchase of the book indicates marketing success. The beauty is, the subject of the book and the process that created it are one and the same. Would you expect anything less when marketing a book with a marketing theme? You shouldn't.

Whether I set out to create a book involving marketing or purely to market a book is also a matter of perspective. Some may believe the intent was to write a book about business and marketing, while others might believe the goal was to create a self-contained marketing case study. Some may even think it was both. In any case, the goals of the book were achieved. Combined with providing an analysis of the political and cultural nuances of business, the book serves as a guide to the most fundamental element of any company or individual's success: The creation and refinement of a product.

I hope you found some of the insights valuable. I also hope you enjoyed the experience.

Until next time.

That's right, next time. Enron made sure of that.

About the Author

The artwork in the background titled *Into The Arena*, depicts a boxer preparing for battle. To Tony, it is symbolic of the psychological preparation needed to enter the *arena* of business management.

During his 27-year career, Tony Paradiso has held senior-level marketing positions with some of the world's most innovative companies. He has spearheaded the marketing efforts for no less than eight market leaders and has helped pioneer such technologies as PCs, videoconferencing, imaging, and handhelds. With a desire to create a different kind of consulting company and obtain the flexibility necessary to pursue a writing career, he founded Paramar Consulting. His consulting services have been retained by the *business elite*, including Intel, AT&T, Soros, and Xerox to name a few.

Tony will be the first to tell you, as important, he has also seen what can cause organizations to stumble, having been involved with companies who have lost once dominant market positions. Being *in the trenches* and witnessing both the ups and downs, has armed Tony with the knowledge of what works and what doesn't.

This real-world experience, combined with his academic accomplishments including graduating with honors with an undergraduate degree in Computer Management from Fordham University and an MBA from Pepperdine University, has provided him with the extensive background that serves as the foundation for this book.

WHAT'S NEXT

The Management Mind Field represents his first book but it won't be his last. The mismanagement demonstrated by Enron validates the views espoused here and Tony is working on a follow-on that will again apply his unique perspective. It promises to be an entertaining *no holds barred* analysis of the root causes of Enron's collapse.

OUR WEB SITE

Tony also publishes a weekly column along with business related opinion/white papers on the Paramar Consulting Web site. Visit **www.paramarconsulting.com** and see what he has to say on topics ranging from business, to sports, to politics.

Acknowledgments

Numerous people unselfishly provided their assistance to help write this book. Without their input, it would have never moved beyond the *experimental* stage.

Most of all, I have to thank my better half, Martine, for putting up with me and my lack of income during the process. The act of writing is a psychologically rewarding experience, but while immersed in it, little income is generated. I thank Martine for both her emotional and financial support. Now that the project is complete, I hope to repay her patience.

Among the many who provided input, I would like to offer my special thanks to Ron and Nancy Anderson. Without their guidance early in the writing process, there is no telling what this book would have become.

Those who lived through the editing process and provided invaluable input include Peg Berry, Jan Cunningham, Don Field, Kevin Flanagan, Brad Freeburg, Joanne Guarino, Cliff Haas, Dean Hough, Sean MacAllister, Betty Meltzer, Genny Ortegon, Angelo Paradiso, Peter Paradiso, Mark Reid, Rick Serodio, Jack Smith, Mike Smith, Genelle Trader, and Brian Yorke.

I'd also like to thank Marlitt Dellabough for her usual first class work on designing the book and Judi Gardner for her professional editing expertise.

Order Form

Order by Fax: Fax this completed form to 603 672 5772.

Order by Phone: Call Paramar Consulting at 603 673 3459.

                     Please have your credit card ready.

Order Online: Go to www.paramarconsulting.com/store/

Order by Mail :   Mail this completed form to:

                     Paramar Consulting

                     P.O. Box 178

                     Amherst, NH 03031

Please include me on your mailing list:

Name: ....

Address: ....

City: .... State: .... Zip Code: ....

Telephone: ....

e-mail: ....

Shipping and Handling

Within the United States: Add $4.00 for the first book and $2 for each additional book.

Outside the United States: Add $10.00 for the first book and $5 for each additional book.

Note: International orders can only be accepted using a credit card.

Payment type: .... Check .... Credit Card

                   .... Visa .... MasterCard .... American Express .... Discover

Card Number: ....

Name on card: ....

Expiration date: ....